ALL PHYSICIANS ARE LEADERS

REFLECTIONS ON INSPIRING CHANGE TOGETHER FOR BETTER HEALTHCARE

Peter B. Angood, MD, FAAPL(Hon)

American Association for
**PHYSICIAN
LEADERSHIP**

PUBLISHER
Nancy Collins

EDITORIAL ASSISTANT
Jennifer Weiss

SEO & CONTENT SPECIALIST
Shannon Lumpkin

DESIGN & LAYOUT
Carter Publishing Studio

COPYEDITOR
Karen Doyle

DEDICATION

To my wonderful family across our generations—
before, now, and in the future. It is said that family
means all; I now believe that entirely!

Thank you all . . . but especially Olivia and Bryanna

TABLE OF CONTENTS

Acknowledgements

This is probably the most treacherous portion of any writing—who and who not to acknowledge? Without doubt, there are always so many others behind any writer, and my situation is no different. I will, therefore, endeavor to not fall into a trap in either direction by not naming specifics.

Family, friends, partners, peers, mentors, teachers, faculty, staff, prior Board members, and even the occasional passersby all deserve credit in some fashion. Thank you to one-and-all, even if you don't recognize how you might have contributed—I know, however, and am deeply appreciative.

The American Association for Physician Leadership® (AAPL) is an incredible organization in so many under-appreciated ways. It is also surprisingly subtle in its own complexity. The AAPL Board of Directors are amazing in their support and encouragement. The AAPL staff at all levels are equally amazing in how their dedication comes through in so many ways as they help deliver the AAPL suite of offerings. They have transformed countless lives in ways they will never be able to quantify. In particular, the AAPL "Chiefs" have contributed to my own growth and development while they so professionally helped shape the course and direction of AAPL over these several recent years—just wow, really! To each of you on these various teams, I cannot thank you enough for all your contributions and commitments to the association, and to me personally. You are each so special.

And yes, I actually have to name a few specifically. Nancy Collins, with her expert team of editors, designers, and publication assistants, was pivotal in helping bring this book to life. Your encouragement, direction, and refinements were so expertly performed that I did not fully appreciate how much naiveté I actually carried until we moved along with the project. Thanks so much for everything! Simone Leite, with support from her entire governance team, has kept me on the straight and true for many years now. Your attention to detail, your humor, and an ability to anticipate what I needed in my professional life without asking has been phenomenal in a host of ways. I cannot thank you enough—really!

Ida Covi is a transformational leader in her own right. For me, your eclectic life trajectory has been something to behold in wonderment, and I am highly privileged to share a deep portion of my life with you. Every day there is some new something I learn, and from which I grow always. You are a treasure, and I look forward to many more experiences in life as we explore the numerous opportunities our lives will offer up as we move along with our family. Love you and thank you for everything you bring to all of our lives.

Dr. Peter B. Angood

About the Author

Peter B. Angood, MD, FRCS(C), FACS, MCCM, FAAPL(Hon)

Dr. Peter Angood has provided senior executive leadership for all sizes and types of healthcare organizations. Since 2012, he has been Chief Executive Officer and President of the American Association for Physician Leadership® (formerly ACPE, American College of Physician Executives); the only professional association solely focused on leadership education, management training, and providing full-service career development offerings oriented toward the physician workforce and the organizations where physicians work or are represented. AAPL is a 45-year-old organization that now has membership in over 40 countries.

Previously Dr. Angood was the inaugural Chief Patient Safety Officer and a Vice-President for The Joint Commission, where he oversaw the National Patient Safety Goals and other enterprise-wide, international patient safety initiatives. He also completed a two-year engagement with the National Quality Forum and National Priorities Partnership as Senior Advisor for Patient Safety before assuming the role of Chief Medical Officer with the Patient Safety Organization of GE Healthcare. During these engagements, Dr. Angood continued intermittent work with the WHO Patient Safety initiative after helping lead early development of the WHO Collaborating Center for Patient Safety Solutions.

Earlier in his career, after initially practicing with hospitals of the McGill University system, Dr. Angood was subsequently recruited to surgery faculty and hospital administrative positions with institutions such as the University of Pennsylvania, Yale University, and Washington University in St. Louis. He completed his formal academic career as a Full Professor of Surgery, Anesthesia, and Emergency Medicine. Dr. Angood is a Fellow of the Royal College of Surgeons

(Canada), the American College of Surgeons. and the American College of Critical Care Medicine, which also recognized him as a Master of Critical Care Medicine. He has a history of active involvement with numerous professional organizations and served as president for the Society of Critical Care Medicine. Dr. Angood's research interests have addressed leading-edge problems; he has authored over 200 publications of varying types and is a well-recognized international speaker on the host of issues related to physician leadership. Dr. Angood is a Fellow of the Explorers Club in New York City.

Dr. Angood received his medical degree from the University of Manitoba in Canada and completed his general surgery training at McGill University in Montreal, as well as fellowship training in trauma surgery and critical care medicine at the University of Miami/Jackson Memorial Hospital in Miami.

Dr. Peter Angood can be contacted at peter.angood@physician leaders.org and at www.physicianleaders.org.

Introduction

A t some level, *all* physicians are considered leaders, and society still has this expectation.

I routinely make this statement because our profession continues to be highly trusted and favorably viewed as a leadership profession. Physicians carry a unique privilege in being able to serve patients and to pursue the public's best interests. Essential for society, we must therefore continue to meet the responsibility of that professional privilege. Leadership is an essential and critical component within this responsibility and set of professional expectations.

Our industry is complex and will remain so for generations to come. In its essence, arguably, U.S. healthcare is still a free-market economy. There are numerous sectors inside the industry, including federal and state governments, each creating influence of varying degree. Within all countries actually, regardless of payment models, these sectors also compete for influence and success. For example, academia and basic science research continue to expand the scientific knowledge of medicine at rapid rates, while technology, pharmaceuticals, device innovation, and digital communication all create equally competing influences. As a result, both physicians and the public now perpetually must balance their expectations for the traditional patient-physician relationship with the rapid pace of change and complexity of the industry. In reality, as each sector attempts to demonstrate its importance, there exists a host of pressures exerted on the industry that may or may not have demonstrable positive impacts on care delivery.

For several decades now, physicians have been primarily focused upon the quickly changing trends in clinical care. We all know the rapid dissemination of medical knowledge is difficult to keep pace with, and evolving technologies make this even more complicated. In addition, there is not only progressive implementation of expanded responsibilities for non-physician providers, but now there is also an expanded number of non-physician clinician types involved with patient care. Which trends in clinical care, in addition to measurement and reporting of clinical outcomes, are most relevant? Who should have the dominant influence on direct patient care?

Several components of a new paradox are gradually becoming clearer—the paradox between existing delivery systems oriented toward how altruistic physicians prefer to deliver care versus a renewed focus on patient-centered care that is trying to thrive in a highly complex set of evolving technology-based systems amidst new types of providers not yet fully oriented to patients.

While patient-centered care is taking on new meaning, the primary focus on physicians being the dominant conduit for care and decision-making remains. As physicians, regardless of chosen discipline, we frequently become embroiled in our patients' lives as they learn about fresh medical uncertainty arriving unwanted into their lives. Certainly, the profession continues to be viewed as the most trusted and highly regarded of all professions. Therefore, the importance of the influence created by physician leadership, as it specifically relates to the patient-physician relationship, is critical for successful relationships at both the direct patient and the organizational levels.

Physicians are granted licensure on the understanding that they will use their knowledge and skills to meet and advance the needs of their patients and, in so doing, place those needs ahead of other considerations, most notably self-interest. The compact thus formed engenders trust among the medical profession, patients, and society. The American Association for Physician Leadership (AAPL) delivers on this expectation of trust and expertise by maximizing the potential of physician leadership to help create significant personal and organizational transformation that benefits patient outcomes and improves healthcare internationally.

Since its founding in 1975 as the American College of Physician Executives, AAPL is the only professional organization solely focused on leadership education, management training, and providing full-service career development offerings oriented toward the physician workforce and the organizations where physicians work or are represented. Additionally, its robust portfolio of information resources is unparalleled . . . and continually growing. And finally (but not the least), the networking community of AAPL is bonded together with a custom-designed and -built technology platform that serves as the glue for all that AAPL provides across its deep catalog of programs, products, and services—also containing an unparalleled suite of resource tools.

Beyond the thousands of physicians who receive training annually, the Association has approximately 250,000 physicians listed in its database who represent a full spectrum of physicians in all forms of leadership roles located in nearly 50 countries. The ever-expanding portfolio of the Association currently includes over 100 courses, numerous certificate and academy offerings, seven Masters degree programs, and deep layers of specialized career-enhancement programs customized for physicians. The industry-standard credential—*Certified Physician Executive (CPE)*—originated with AAPL in 1997.

I am distinctly privileged to help lead this 45-year-old association. In this role, I routinely encourage physicians to continue seeking deeper levels of professional development throughout their career trajectory—and to appreciate better how we can each generate positive influence at all levels in our industry. As physician leaders, we must be more engaged, stay engaged, and help others to become engaged. Creating a broader level of positive change in healthcare—and society—is within our reach. Our patients and their families will clearly appreciate the eventual outcome.

This book of personal reflections on healthcare and the state of our industry is, just that, personal. I am deeply humbled that others so strongly encouraged me to bring this collection to publication in book format. I can only hope that as one reads the various passages, it might cause further personal reflection while also instilling, perhaps, a renewed sense of privilege and commitment to the profession. Being a leader, as a physician in our society, is unique and carries far broader degrees of influence than we can ever appreciate—try not to miss your opportunity.

INSPIRING CHANGE. TOGETHER.

CHAPTER 1

All Physicians Are Leaders ...at Some Level

Understanding change is the key to accepting and engaging in it. Physicians can get more engaged, stay engaged, and help others become engaged. Creating a broader level of positive change in healthcare is within your capability, if you so choose.

A ll physicians are considered leaders . . . at some level. Whether we recognize it or not, physicians are always being looked upon in this regard. Our society certainly continues to expect the profession's members to provide representative leadership. As individuals, physicians also provide leadership within our professional, personal, and community activities on a routine basis. Leadership is what our profession has demonstrated in society for numerous generations, and it is expected to continue doing so for the foreseeable future.

With the ongoing changes in healthcare, physician leadership is now more topical and important than ever before. Regardless of whether it is formal or informal, traditional or non-traditional, one does not necessarily need to be in an organizational leadership role to provide leadership.

As one considers their evolving understanding of leadership and the potential roles they may want to explore, it is important to recognize how one's skills are viewed in the marketplace (Figure 1.1). Ralph Roberto of Keystone Partners once helped me appreciate the

Changing Skill Requirements

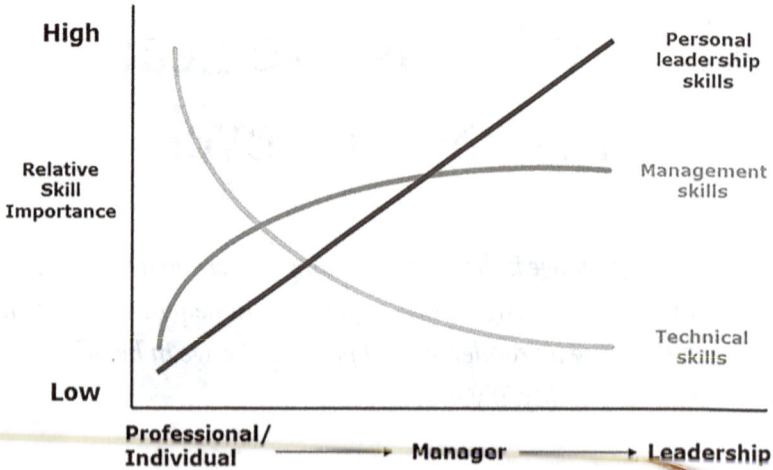

FIGURE 1.1. Changing Skill Requirements for Physician Leaders

metaphor of managing your personal financial portfolio with leadership. In terms of your own career, everyone needs to regularly review their current assets and liabilities, their professional goals, a realistic time horizon, and their action plan; and certainly undergo an annual review with rebalancing of assets. In so doing, he also reiterated that the number one factor that differentiates successful leaders is their ability to gain useful feedback and then to act upon it constructively.

Physicians often miss out on the importance of taking these steps due to the busy-ness of their practices and not having been advised on the importance of these considerations.

Figure 1.2 presents a useful graphic when determining the strength and relevance of your own assets as you move toward formal leadership roles, remembering, of course, that leadership also occurs without being engaged in formal positions or traditional clinical practice. It is a core of what we physicians do.

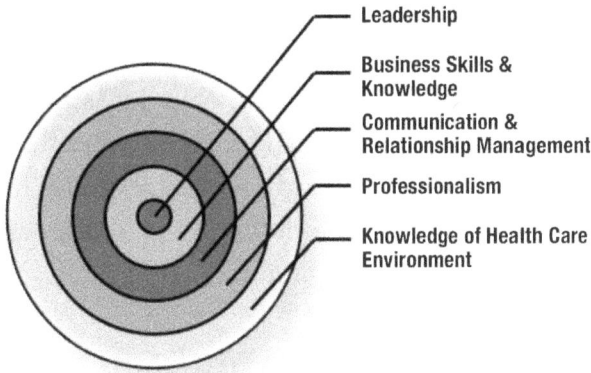

- Leadership
- Business Skills & Knowledge
- Communication & Relationship Management
- Professionalism
- Knowledge of Health Care Environment

FIGURE 1.2. Leadership is the Bullseye

As Figure 1.2 depicts, leadership is the bullseye for all physicians, and moving toward that bullseye can be viewed as a gradual maturing of skills from the outer edges of the target to the inner core. Obviously this is only one depiction, and it could also be easily presented, for example, as an overlapping series of inter-dependent Venn diagram circles. The overall point being, however, that we as physicians need to pay attention to these competencies as we move along our career trajectories.

And my underlying point remains: that all physicians are considered leaders at some level.

Across multiple types of practice environments, physician-led healthcare provides improved outcomes, quality, safety, and efficiency. Yes, the environment of healthcare is rapidly changing, but the vast majority of healthcare is still provided under direction from physicians.

IN HEALTHCARE, THE ONLY CONSTANT IS CHANGE

"Healthcare is undergoing profound change, and we need to be ready." I was musing with someone recently how, in some fashion, this phrase has been circulating for the better part of our careers.

I graduated from medical school in 1981 and remember hearing about the needed changes for healthcare then. I also remember commenting to a senior faculty person while I was a surgery resident about how I thought his generation had it better than our coming generation. Interestingly, his immediate response was, "Actually, Peter, I think the generation before mine had it perfectly." Over the years there have been numerous other examples for me as well.

THE GRASS IS ALWAYS GREENER

Physicians care deeply about patients and people in general. We proudly wear our altruism and idealism on our sleeves. And yes, at times, the grass can be greener elsewhere. But in our drive toward greener grass, we continually seek ways to better manage or control our environments.

This is often an inherent component of physician personalities. Sometimes we succeed in our efforts with managing the circumstances, while at others we become frustrated and even demoralized.

Nonetheless, doing what is best for patients remains a core belief and an essential beacon of stability in healthcare. From my perspective, students and trainees of today continue with that same sense of value—perhaps even stronger than prior generations.

STILL HUMAN

The paradox is this, however: human beings are human beings, and our core physiologic, biochemical, and biological processes do not change that drastically over relatively short periods of time. Yes, the general health and welfare of people gradually changes, and the evolution of disease states also gradually change over time. But none of those changes is rapid, and it takes decades, generations, or even centuries for the changes to become evident. Human beings are, after all, human beings. So where is all the change coming from? A short list includes:

- Improved basic understanding of our biology and physiology;
- Development of better pharmacologics and medical devices;
- An appreciation that focusing on preventive health may be a preferred approach to managing disease states;
- Recognition that supporting sciences such as epidemiology and biostatistics can refine our understanding; and
- The realization that implementing a continuum-of-care approach will provide improved health and better patient outcomes.

The potentially more frustrating arenas of change for physicians, however, are not those related to the historical approaches for improving the science of medicine. They are changes imposed on the delivery of care because of:

- Increasing presence of political and policy engagement with healthcare;
- Escalating regulatory and oversight burdens;
- Expanding sets of inexact measures and flawed reporting efforts;
- Routine shifting of risk management and expense burdens;
- Ongoing uncertainty with the legal environment and future approaches within healthcare; and
- Poorly aligned financial models that routinely confuse all participants in the industry.

Again, this is just a short list. With all three components taken together, the varying paces of change are a fourth contributing factor. While the evolution of human beings and disease states is slower, the exciting pace of change with science and technology continues to rapidly gain momentum at unprecedented levels.

EMBRACING CHANGE

But it is the speed of change; the courses of change in health services delivery models; and the rapidly shifting policy, financial, or legal reform approaches that I hear about from physicians. The frustration with these changes is difficult to manage because these are areas in which physicians are not routinely provided the background education or opportunity to easily gain further knowledge and understanding.

When not able to understand, physicians can become discouraged with change. There is no inherent resistance to change itself, but more to the difficulty in knowing how to adapt and adjust to change when the circumstances or the environment are uncertain and unpredictable.

In reality, physicians often are proud of the ability to flex, change, and innovate.

I remain quite impressed with how the physician workforce has become more engaged with learning how to adjust and participate constructively with the change in healthcare at all levels. Physicians are making significant impacts across a host of environments. Positive change is happening as a result of physician engagement. I hear this frequently.

Ultimately, our overriding purpose is to be able to generate change toward exceptional healthcare delivery through physician leadership. In so doing, healthcare organizations of all types can benefit with more efficient, streamlined, high-quality systems of care, and overall health for patients will be improved.

We are indeed in a state of perpetual change for the industry. But this is a critically important period in healthcare because it is being recognized and appreciated that physician leadership is pivotal for driving successful change in healthcare at all levels.

Chapter 2

Physicians, Value, and Compound Interest: Benefits of a Physician-Led Organization

The expectation for value in healthcare is changing. Just as compound interest adds value to a bank account, strong physician leadership can do the same for healthcare organizations.

Most of us know the value equation for its simplicity:

$$Value = Quality/Cost$$

With current trends, stakeholders throughout the healthcare system increasingly recognize the need for greater value in healthcare—improvements in both the quality and cost of care. The emergence of new value-based care and payment models also emphasizes the importance of collaboration between the physician and financial leaders within healthcare organizations.

From my vantage point, it is incumbent for each of us to seek ways that encourage and refine our relationships with financial leaders. Healthcare and patient care will benefit greatly.

While doing so, it is imperative that leaders communicate a common message about the pursuit of value, which requires a common definition and agreement on the metrics selected to track progress.

Distinct capabilities in four categories can help organizations navigate the shifts required to move toward value-based care delivery:

1. People and culture;
2. Business intelligence;
3. Performance improvement; and
4. Contract and risk management.

One powerful concept that can help bridge the traditional gap between physician and financial leaders is the goal of becoming a high-reliability organization: one that delivers performance as intended consistently over time. This consistency would translate into:

- No harm to patients (safety focus);
- Clinical excellence (quality focus);
- Patient satisfaction (patient-centered care); and
- Positive margin (financial focus).

Organizational leaders can use the so-called "trust cycle" to enable the changes required for successful adoption of new care and payment models. The cycle includes four key steps:

1. Finding common ground;
2. Having needed dialogues that are healthy, meaningful, and safe;
3. Tapping collective wisdom; and
4. Building trust.

COST AND QUALITY

Because the transition to value-based models inherently includes quality and cost, it is critical for clinical and financial leaders to collaborate. It is important to acknowledge that chief medical officers (CMOs) and chief financial officers (CFOs) speak different languages, have different perspectives and focus on different goals. It is absolutely key for physician and financial leaders to recognize and understand the characteristics of their colleagues in the C-suite.

Success in the value-based environment requires leaders who can bridge the gaps between the clinical and financial realms. It requires physician leaders who can understand finances and can galvanize their peers around organizational or population health goals. Success also requires financial leaders who understand clinical priorities. CFOs must be able to identify relevant, actionable data for physicians and to communicate effectively with CMOs and care providers.

It is essential that organizations minimize dollars withheld from penalty programs and maximize dollars received in reimbursement or incentive programs. Financial success in these programs requires physician and financial leaders who have a clear understanding of the various payment programs and a process for shifting strategies and practices in response to changes in these programs.

The availability of timely, accurate, actionable data is vitally important to providing the feedback that clinical and financial leaders need to navigate the transition from volume-based to value-based payment. It is also essential for providing rapid feedback and comparative dashboards to align frontline physicians with organizational goals and make informed decisions that affect population health.

Issues with interoperability and difficulties with amassing data from different IT systems when inconsistencies are present remain significant barriers to optimal data sharing. Together, we can better pressure the IT industry to resolve these inconsistencies more rapidly.

Finally, the vast amount of data collected requires translation to usable information for other leaders, clinicians and patients. Leaders must ensure that all required metrics are collected and reported yet identify the "meta-drivers"—those key levers for optimizing performance with which incentives should be aligned.

COMPOUND INTEREST

So where does the concept of compound interest come in to play?

Compound interest can be thought of as "interest on interest." It is the interest amount calculated on the initial principal and also on the accumulated interest of previous periods of a deposit or loan. It will make a deposit or loan grow at a faster rate than simple interest, which is interest calculated only on the principal amount. In fact, the magic of compounding apparently led to the apocryphal story of Albert Einstein supposedly calling it the eighth wonder of the world and/or man's greatest invention.[1]

Paul Keckley, PhD, a renowned healthcare economist and thought leader, has stated, "Chief medical officers are the MVPs in most health care organizations. Getting the right individual in the role is perhaps the most important decision a CEO makes. Getting it wrong can threaten the sustainability of the organization."

Within this changing healthcare environment, successful physician leadership can be considered essential because well-educated physician leaders are ideally positioned to leverage the interface between the clinical and business realms of healthcare.

Physician leaders can provide valuable insight about the clinical implications of business decisions, guide organizational changes and performance improvement initiatives, and ensure continued prioritization of care quality despite the increased focus on cost and efficiency. They also can successfully advocate for patients, as well as for all types of patient care providers in a balanced fashion.

Effective physician leadership also supports physician career satisfaction and sustainability by enhancing an improved communication between the front lines of care and any health system's administration regarding resource needs, barriers and frustrations in daily practice. Indeed, the benefits of having a physician-run hospital or healthcare system are numerous. These organizations typically:

- Emphasize change management;
- Have a better understanding on nature of challenges and common knowledge base;
- Possess an improved understanding of patient care operational issues;
- Are unwilling to compromise quality/safety/labor for profit;
- View finance as a means not an end;
- Align differing values between clinical professions and have improved interprofessional interactions;
- Place a greater value on physician leadership and compensate appropriately;
- Anticipate change within the healthcare industry and selectively embrace new technologies/methods (e.g., new trends, governmental regulation);
- Are better coordinated with referral sources (private offices/clinic); and
- Have less duplication of similar services within region, more collaboration among local hospitals.

Physician leaders are needed to ensure that patients receive compassionate, high-quality, and safe care, while working to steward precious resources and optimize organizational efficiency and financial viability. For these many reasons, developing physician leaders is key to success in the current healthcare landscape, and will continue to be well into the future.

So, clearly, beyond our clinical expertise, the effect of physician leadership further compounds the benefits of physician engagement and successful patient outcomes within organizations. Organizations that are physician-led (i.e., CEOs, CMOs, etc.) do better in many ways—a compounded benefit well beyond strong clinical care.

Physician leadership is valuable in other ways as well. A survey of physicians conducted by the American Association for Physician

Leadership® found that a majority believe physician leaders are more likely to be able to improve physician satisfaction levels within the profession than non-physician leaders. Further, more than half of the surveyed physicians identified physician leadership as being key to generating success within their organizations.

Leadership, both formal and informal, is a lifelong learning process. With the vast majority of healthcare still delivered, or directly supervised by physicians, the physician workforce is still optimally placed to help bridge the gap to a better healthcare system. A system that drives value to patients and organizations; one that is highly efficient, safe and with measurement that is able to effectively demonstrate optimal quality of care.

At some level, all physicians can be considered leaders. Compound your value—to yourself and to your organization.

REFERENCE

5. Investopedia.com. investopedia.com/terms/c/compoundinterest.asp.

CHAPTER 3

Demographics, Shifting Models, and Physician Leadership

Within the current era of physician workforce changes there are opportunities for physician leadership. Concern is related to the projected physician shortage, the growing and aging population, and competing population health needs.

Statistics from the Federation of State Medical Boards from 2018 show that there are 985,026 licensed physicians in the US.[1]

With an average age of 51.5 years, 74.5% are certified by an American Board of Medical Specialties Specialty Board, and a large majority is licensed in a single state (78.4%). While two thirds of physicians are still male, the recognized changing demographic at the medical school level is now beginning to be noticed at the licensure level. And 33.1% of female physicians are less than 39 years old compared with only 19.2% of male physicians.[1]

With 30.3% of physicians now over age 60 years, up from 25.2% in 2010, there is clearly a demonstrable actuarial need for an increased supply of physicians in order to avert a physician manpower shortage in the near future.[1]

Generally consistent with previous reports it has issued, an analysis in 2019 by the Association of American Medical Colleges (AAMC) projects a shortage of between 46,900 to 121,900 physicians by 2032.[2]

Much of the projected shortage and concern is related to the growing and aging population, reflecting both the increasing healthcare needs of older individuals as well as the practice patterns of aging physicians, who may work fewer hours or retire. Younger physicians, too, may be working fewer hours as they seek a better work-life balance.[2]

According to the U.S. Census Bureau, the year 2030 will mark an important demographic shift in the U.S. population, when all baby boomers (individuals born between 1946 and 1964) will be older than 65 years of age. By 2035, for the first time in U.S. history, adults 65 years and older are also projected to outnumber children under 18 years of age.[3]

Discussion and debate surrounding adequate provision of healthcare continues to escalate regarding implementation of the federal Affordable Care Act (ACA). The ACA will continue to expand coverage over the next few years. This plus an aging population further compounds the need for increased physician manpower coverage. The AAMC states that physician shortage numbers will increase to greater than 120,000 during the next 10 years.[2]

Additionally, distribution between physician generalist and specialist disciplines continues to be disproportionate and the preferences among physician choices for specialties are non-uniform in relation to population needs. There are also recognized trends in physician preference toward employed compensation arrangements and so-called controllable lifestyles. Two trends especially prevalent in younger generation physicians.[4,5]

Within the current era of these physician workforce changes and competing population health needs, however, there are significant evolving models of care delivery and financial payments. The various initiatives around Accountable Care Organizations and the move toward value-based payment (VBP) models being most notable these days. Newer models for medical homes and specialty medical homes are also gradually finding their way into the healthcare marketplace as a result of opportunities created with a changing landscape. And for all, to be competitive under value-based business models, hospitals (and practices) should build meaningful scale and scope, while also focusing on physician integration, costs, quality of care, and customer service.[6]

From my perspective, the traditional healthcare value equation of Value = Quality/Cost now clearly needs to also include, at the very least, Access and Efficiency in that equation.

$$Value = Quality/Cost + Access + Efficiency$$

And for our traditional models of health system—academic medical centers, aligned integrated systems, multi-hospital systems, rural hospitals, and stand-alone hospitals—in addition to the wide variety of physician practice models, all are necessarily included in the evolving requirements for meeting these shifting needs.[7]

Interestingly, in 2013 Kaiser Health News (KHN) reported that physician-owned hospitals continue to emerge as among the biggest winners under two programs in the health law. One rewards or penalizes hospitals based on how well they score on quality measures. The other penalizes hospitals where too many patients are readmitted after they leave.[8] There are now more than 260 hospitals owned by doctors scattered around 33 states (especially prevalent in Texas, Louisiana, Oklahoma, California and Kansas) according to Physician Hospitals of America, a trade group.[9]

Of 161 physician-owned hospitals that were eligible to participate in the health law's quality programs, 122 received extra money, and 39 lost funds, the KHN analysis shows, in contrast with other hospitals where 74% were penalized. Medicare is paying the average physician-owned hospital bonuses of 0.21% more for each patient during the fiscal year that runs through September, the analysis found. Meanwhile, the average hospital not run by doctors lost 0.30% per Medicare patient.

Past research has shown that physician-owned hospitals score highly in following basic clinical guidelines and pleasing patients—the same factors that Medicare is using to determine bonuses and penalties in its VBP program. These successes are arguably made easier by the fact that many patients come to these facilities for elective surgeries rather than emergencies, allowing for more orderly preparations than at a typical acute-care hospital.

Having spent more than 25 years of my career in academic safety-net institutions, I don't necessarily ascribe to physician-owned hospitals as the optimal model of care—and they do generate heated discussion among policymakers—but an argument can certainly be made that engagement of physicians and integration of physician leadership are critical for optimal success to occur in the development of these various evolving models. Why? Because physician leadership is able to provide deep and mature levels of insight on the clinical delivery side as well as on the administrative side within healthcare.

PHYSICIAN LEADERSHIP AND HOSPITAL PERFORMANCE: IS THERE AN ASSOCIATION?

Among the nearly 6500 hospitals in the United States, only 235 are run by physicians, but the overall hospital quality scores are 25% higher when doctors run hospitals,[7] compared with other hospitals.[9]

Overall, the complexity for managing these various trends is therefore intuitively difficult and obviously creates many challenges. While moderating a panel at the World Health Care Congress 2013 on "Bending the Cost Curve," I appreciated there was clear recognition that while these fluxes and shifts within healthcare are complex, opportunity is still available in abundance to help create positive change. Strong common agreement with the panelists and audience was that in leveraging opportunity, care must continue to focus on being patient-centered. As well, general agreement demonstrated that all types of entities engaged with the healthcare industry must continue to invest in innovation and innovative approaches to these models and systems of care provision. Transparency of efforts, a degree of crowdsourcing on difficult problems, and an increase with proactive collaboration across sectors of the industry will also continue to emerge as important trends.

REFERENCES

1. Young A, Chaudhry HJ, Pei X, et al. FSMB Census of Licensed Physicians in the United States, 2018. *Journal of Medical Regulation.* 2019;105(2);7-23. www.fsmb. org/siteassets/advocacy/publications/2018census.pdf.

2. Association of American Medical Colleges. 2019 Update: The complexities of physician supply and demand: projections from 2017 to 2032. 2019. https://aamc-black. global.ssl.fastly.net/production/media/filer_public/31/13/3113ee5c-a038-4c16-89af-294a69826650/2019_update_-_the_complexities_of_physician_supply_and_ demand_-_projections_from_2017-2032.pdf.

3. U.S. Census Bureau. Older people projected to outnumber children for first time in U.S. history. 2018. https://www.census.gov/newsroom/pressreleases/2018/ cb18-41-population-projections.html.

4. AAMC. Center for Workforce Shortage Studies, 2010. https://www.aamc.org.

5. Kocher R, Sahni NR. Hospitals' race to employ physicians: the logic behind a money-losing proposition. *New Engl J Med.* 2011;364:1790-1793.

6. Healthcare Financial Management. November 2012. https://hfma.org.

7. Parker-Pope T. Should hospitals be run by doctors? Well Blog, New York Times. July 7, 2011. https://well.blogs.nytimes.com/2011/07/07/should-hospitals-be-run-by-doctors/.

8. Rau J. Doctor-owned hospitals prosper under health law. Kaiser Health News. April 12, 2013. https://khn.org/news/doctor-owned-hospitals-quality-bonuses/.

9. Goodall AH. Physician-leaders and hospital performance: is there an association? Soc Sci Med. 73(4):535-539, August 2011.

CHAPTER 4

Competencies and Lifelong Learning

Learning is a lifelong process. Not all learning needs to be in formalized education programs, however. Professionally, medical education has long duration, is usually organized, and at times is quite arduous. In contrast, on a personal level, our learning is much more spontaneous and unexpected, often covering areas where we are not enlightened with how best to proceed (e.g., raising children). Continuous professional development often falls in the zone of something we must do. We should, nonetheless, seek it enthusiastically so that we remain competent and professionally expert. This latter arena is indeed our committed area of expertise.

Remember the first time you heard it? Its potential was thrilling on the one hand yet terrifying on the other. The first step was easy (supposedly), the second step was more complex to achieve (successfully), and the third step carried an aura of expertise (albeit a falsehood).

Figured it out? Of course, it's: *See One, Do One, Teach One.*

Gives me the shivers just thinking about it actually. Being procedurally oriented as a surgeon, I recall many instances during training and in the early stages of my career when that scenario played itself out. Thankfully, I don't remember experiencing any bad outcomes or significant errors, but I am aware of many unfortunate situations for others.

Genesis of The Expert

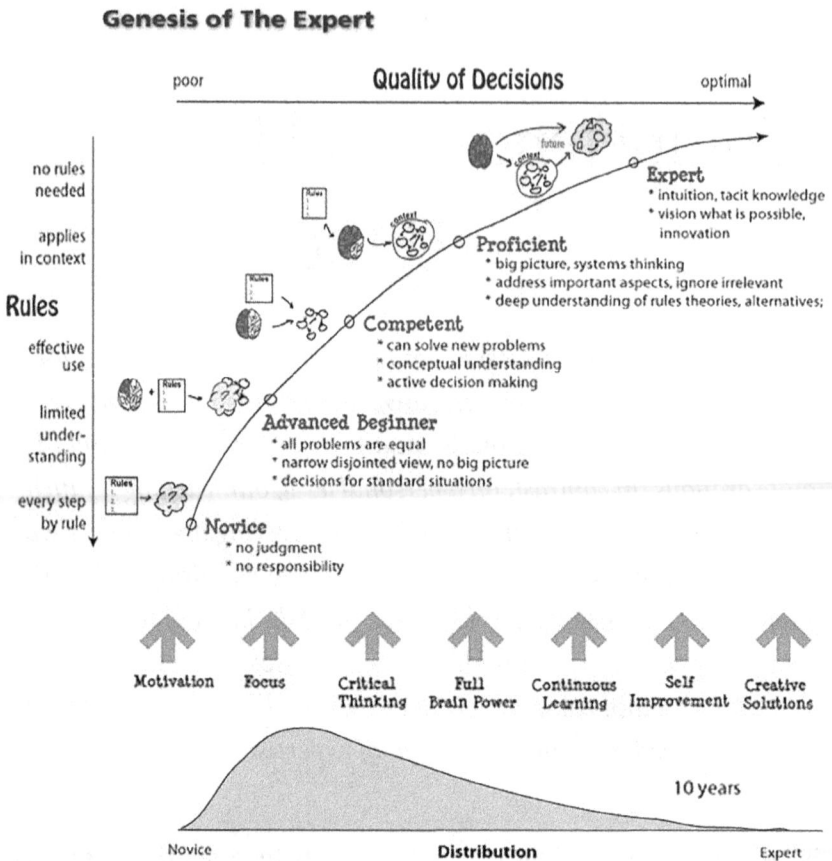

FIGURE 4.1. Genesis of the expert. From (1).

Most of us are able to progress along the trajectory from novice in our chosen clinical specialty to recognized expert. The timeframe to accomplish this gradual maturation varies for many reasons, but the average is usually around 10 years or about 10,000 hours of focused effort on an area of specific talent, if you happen to believe that theory (Figure 4.1).

And yet, just when you think you are a so-called master, something happens that reminds you that learning is a lifelong process. Humility can be a rude lesson to learn.

Can we harness similar principles for leadership? Is one individual able to become a *master leader*? It is a question that already has a deep, rich literature and a plethora of theories to debate:

- **Continuous Professional Development:** If we are going to improve healthcare, continuous professional development cannot be just for individuals—it must include organizations as well. Working collaboratively across all the industry sectors is essential for success.

- **Competency-Based Learning:** Competency-based learning has become an essential cornerstone not only in educational theory but also within educational practices. This type of learning is especially critical for professions such as medicine and has been integrated in both medical school curricula and residency training programs for some time, albeit not yet across all institutions.

Competency is a cluster of related abilities, commitments, knowledge, and skills that enable a person (or an organization) to act effectively in a job or situation.[2] Competence indicates sufficiency of knowledge and skills that enable someone to act in a wide variety of situations. This can occur in any period of a person's life or at any stage of his or her career.

Physicians much embrace defensible, industry-recognized competencies that are backed by scientific instrumentation and research. The complementary blend of leadership characteristics and technical skills combine to create the AAPL holistic competency model for physician leadership (see sidebar on AAPL holistic competency model).

By using this combined approach, we more effectively apply a competency-based learning strategy enabling individuals to gradually move through the stages of professional development that mimics novice to expert. There are four leadership growth stages: fundamental, developmental, experiential, and transformational. This gradual growth also creates a progression in how leaders mature in their degree of influence:

AAPL HOLISTIC COMPETENCY MODEL
FOR PHYSICIAN LEADERSHIP

Self-Management

- Self-awareness
- Humility
- Resilience
- Self-control

Professional Capabilities

- Integrity
- Judgment
- Accountability
- Influence

Team Building and Teamwork

- Team building
- Developing relationships
- Collaborative function
- Working with and through others

Problem Solving

- Strategic perspective
- Conflict management
- Action orientation
- Critical appraisal skills

Motivations and Thinking Style

- Motivate others

- Adaptability
- Trust and respect
- Comfort with visibility

Operations and Policy

- Governance
- Communication strategies
- Technology integration
- People management

Quality and Risk

- Quality improvement
- Healthcare process
- Risk management
- Health law

Finance

- Financial management
- Economics
- Resource allocation
- Payment models

Strategy and Innovation

- Performance
- Systems awareness
- Differentiation
- Environmental influences

- **Become a Leader/Influence Yourself:** Influence starts with honest self-awareness. To start the journey toward leadership, you must think about these questions—what are your values, and more importantly, why are they significant to you? Until you answer those, any outward influence you attempt will be imbalanced and ineffective.

- **Lead Your Team/Influence your Team:** Once you've analyzed your own personal values, you're ready to effectively influence others. But to inspire your peers, you need to build relationships—understand the environment in which they operate, and the things that are most important to them.
- **Lead Your Department/Influence Your Department:** When you effectively connect with those around you, you can begin to shape the culture, values and direction of an entire department. Relying on the experience and acumen you've gained from others, you can influence the organization to adopt a new identify and way of thinking.
- **Lead Your Organization/Influence your Organization:** Once people are aligned, they start to generate new ideas and interesting ideas of thought. You can leverage these insights and develop strategies that influence the direction of the whole organization.

All of these eventually will align closely to the same comprehensive set of competencies and instruments to measure accurately and consistently across all types of individual and organizational engagements.

Getting back to the core questions: Can we harness similar principles for leadership? Is one able to become a *master leader?* Facilitating growth of *master physician leaders* is the mission.

There are useful resources for the best approach to this trajectory of thought leadership. The original CanMEDS Physician Competency Framework, developed by the Royal College of Physicians and Surgeons of Canada,[3] has been embraced by many around the world, and it has inspired descriptions for the following roles of physicians:

1. Medical Expert (EXP)
2. Communicator (COM)
3. Collaborator (COL)
4. Leader/Manager (LEA)
5. Health Advocate (ADV)
6. Scholar (SCH)
7. Professional (PRO)

CANMEDS 4: PHYSICIAN LEADER/MANAGER COMPETENCIES 3

4.1 Understand the principles of population medicine and its strategies, and use the main tools which are used in epidemiology and public health. These include the gathering and use of health determinants and indicators, descriptive and explanatory statistics, risk and protective factors and the concepts of prevention and health promotion at individual, community and environmental levels.

4.2 Define and illustrate health promotion and health-enhancing strategies at various levels, such as the monitoring and promotion of a safe environment and the promotion of effective public health policies and interventions. In doing so, they take into account financial, material and staffing resources, at both community and public health levels.

4.3 Recognize and respond to disease outbreaks, epidemics and pandemics.

4.4 Identify and address the special needs of vulnerable populations, showing awareness of the importance of equity in the delivery of care. They seek collaboration with social services if appropriate.

4.5 Address the psychosocial, insurance, financial and environmental aspects of handicaps and chronic diseases.

4.6 Identify the roles and describe the functions of the health and invalidity insurance system and its impact on health and health care at both individual and collective levels.

4.7 Integrate the principles of economic effectiveness and efficiency in daily work and the planning of healthcare provision.

4.8 Identify and engage in opportunities for continuous improvement of the health care system, based on a critical understanding of the continuous transformation of medicine and society.

Category 4, Leader/Manager, for example is described as: "as *managers* and individuals demonstrating leadership, physicians are engaged individuals who take the initiative to contribute in a collaborative way toward positive and sustainable change in health care, from the level of an individual patient to that of the health care system . . ." (See the sidebar on CanMEDS 4.)

ENTRUSTABLE PROFESSIONAL ACTIVITIES

An Entrustable Professional Activity (EPA) is a unit of professional practice defined as a task or responsibility that a trainee is entrusted to perform unsupervised once he or she has attained sufficient competence in the activity.[4] EPAs are context-dependent, which means that EPAs should be taught and applied in common professional situations. It is an essential task of a "discipline" that an individual can be trusted to perform independently in a given context. They are often used for assessment purposes and encompass multiple milestones.

Milestones are then defined as observable markers of an individual's ability along a developmental continuum and can be used for planning or teaching the skills related to an EPA.

The key difference between EPAs and milestones is that EPAs are the tasks or activities that must be accomplished while learning, whereas milestones are the actual abilities of the individual being assessed while learning. The combination of milestones and EPAs allow educators to examine performance at both the micro (when needed) and macro levels, providing a balanced view of trainees' abilities.

How do EPAs differ from competencies?

EPAs are not an alternative for competencies but a means to translate competencies into practice.

- Competencies are descriptors of professionals; EPAs are descriptors of work.
- EPAs usually require multiple competencies in an integrative, holistic nature.
- Confused? For those interested in developing EPAs, Figure 4.2 provides a useful framework.

Physicians are becoming thought leaders and are influencing groups in healthcare. Our responsibility at the AAPL is to further contribute to the academic development of the physician and interprofessional leadership discourse.

1. Title	Make it short; avoid words related to proficiency or skill. Ask yourself: Can a trainee be scheduled to do this? Can an entrustment decision for unsupervised practice for this EPA be made and documented?
2. Description	To enhance universal clarity, include everything necessary to specify the following: What is included? What limitations apply? Limit the description to the actual activity. Avoid justifications of why the EPA is important, or references to knowledge and skills.
3. Required Knowledge, Skills, and Attitudes (KSAs)	Which competency domains apply? Which subcompetencies apply? Include only the most relevant ones. These links may serve to build observation and assessment methods.
4. Required KSAs	Which KSAs are necessary to execute the EPA? Formulate this in a way to set expectations. Refer to resources that reflect necessary or helpful standards (books, a skills course, etc).
5. Information to assess progress	Consider observations, products, monitoring of knowledge and skill, multisource feedback.
6. When is unsupervised practice expected?	Estimate when full entrustment for unsupervised practice is expected, acknowledging the flexible nature of this. Expectations of entrustment moments can shape an individual workplace curriculum.
7. Basis for formal entrustment decisions	How many times must the EPA be executed proficiently for unsupervised practice? Who will judge this? What does formal entrustment look like (documented, publicly announced)?

FIGURE 4.2. Guidelines for Full Entrustable Professional Activities (EPA) Descriptions. From (5).

SITUATIONS AS STARTING POINTS

Because we have been discussing lifelong learning principles, it is important to define starting points. They are "a set of generic situations which cover the common circumstances, symptoms, complaints and findings that a physician should be able to manage clinically."[6]

For instance, *jaundice* may be a starting point for numerous situations such as neonatal jaundice, hepatitis, pancreatic cancer, or cirrhosis. Use of these situations clinically can assist students to develop their skills in clinical reasoning, to increase their ability to integrate various options into their differential diagnosis, and to maintain an interdisciplinary perspective. The situations are also intended to be used by faculty and teachers to illustrate lectures, to engage in problem-based learning sessions and to facilitate bedside teaching.

The professional development field for physicians has its own set of intrigues (think Maintenance of Competence) and continues to remain murky at times.

The potential of physician leadership is to create significant personal and organizational transformation. I encourage each of us to continue seeking deeper levels of professional development and to appreciate better how we can each generate positive influence at all levels.

As physician leaders, let us become more engaged, stay engaged, and help others to become engaged. Creating a broader level of positive change in healthcare—and society—is within our reach. Our patients and their families will appreciate the eventual outcome.

REFERENCES

1. Mapp B. Communication, Thinking, and Learning course. Episode 8, Creating Creation Companies. https://gohighbrow.com/communication-thinking-and-learning.
2. The Business Dictionary. http://www.businessdictionary.com/definition/competence.html.
3. Profiles. General objectives. CanMEDS. www.profilesmed.ch/canmeds.
4. Profiles. Entrustable Professional Activities (EPAs). CanMEDS. www.profilesmed.ch/epas.
5. ten Cate O. Nuts and bolts of Entrustable Professional Activities. *J Grad Med Educ.* 2013;5(1):157-1588.
6. Profiles. Situations as Starting Points (SSPs). CanMEDS. www.profilesmed.ch/ssps.

CHAPTER 5

Safety, Transparency, and Physician Leadership

Approaching transparency while improving patient safety is more complicated than it appears, but physician leadership is essential in helping make it become reality.

A
ttending a high-profile conference on patient safety, I was struck by a few things. First, and most unfortunately, it was a déjà vu experience. Before becoming CEO of the AAPL, I spent many years working in patient safety, nationally and internationally. My déjà vu feeling came from recognizing that more than a decade later I was still hearing essentially the same issues being raised at the conference— the same issues that our healthcare system hasn't been able to solve for years.

Second, a question resurfaced for me: What other industry would consistently tolerate 30% waste and inefficiency coupled with a 10% significant error rate? Yes, U.S. healthcare is essentially a free-market economy, has numerous sectors competing for a portion of that economy, and compared to other industries is relatively unregulated by oversight agencies. Yes, the system has numerous aspects that are the envy of other countries. But as I was reminded again, we still have much to learn and gain in terms of creating large-scale change that will be sustainable over time.

These initial comments should not be construed as another gloom-and-doom piece. By nature, I am optimistic and remain strongly positive on the direction we are headed as these complex issues and problems continue to be addressed. There is much to be proud of within our healthcare system and the collective approaches toward improvement.

However, the current era of efforts toward improved patient safety and higher quality in healthcare is now more than 20 years in the making. Although there are numerous success stories within a host of clinical delivery systems, ongoing disappointment at a macro level persists, and we have not made enough significant progress as quickly as we had hoped.

Collectively, one can recognize that we continue to grapple with core systems-oriented problems that clearly affect the individuals trying to work successfully on care delivery. Progress has been slow, but at least now it is recognizable, and ongoing efforts are becoming more successful. Continuing on the positive side, several secondary aspects related to safety and quality for healthcare have gradually emerged in this evolutionary process of industry change. We can and do continue to learn from other industries while we also continue to grasp the concepts of implementing innovation better at system levels. This has been critically important for our industry to appreciate.

Nonetheless, in my opinion, how we create ongoing change for healthcare will be contingent on creating systems and processes designed by expert healthcare providers that are appropriately relevant for delivering positive change in healthcare delivery—especially for patients, families and individual providers.

TRANSPARENCY MATTERS

An important aspect to focus on is transparency. We all recognize how the healthcare industry primarily has revolved for decades around the knowledge and decision-making of physicians. The shift from a traditionally paternalistic approach by physicians toward truly patient-centered care with shared decision-making is certainly underway—and appropriately so.

Inevitably though, errors occur and will continue to occur during clinical care. Therefore, an important related aspect of shared decision-making also is sharing of information on processes and outcomes of care, regardless of their nature.

With all physicians considered as leaders at some level, do we truly understand and fully appreciate the pivotal importance of transparency for physician leadership? Additionally, the perspective on what constitutes transparency can be highly variable. The patients' perspective? Physicians? Other providers? Health systems and hospitals? Risk managers and our legal system? The general public and lay media?

Further, the infrastructure required to support effective transparency and the complexity of processes for interdisciplinary cooperation that assures transparency across the various sectors of the industry are a heavier burden than initially appreciated.

When all is functioning smoothly and outcomes are optimal, then transparency is easy. When errors or glitches happen and less optimal outcomes are generated, then system fault lines are exposed. Communications are derailed if a transparency system and culture have not been adequately designed or implemented. Animosity, even hostility, may be a result.

Transparency is much more than sharing positive information or providing an apology with disclosure when a negative outcome occurs. Physicians play a vital role in setting expectations for themselves and the systems in which they practice. Our inputs are critical for designing, implementing and maintaining effective systems for ensuring transparency across the continuum of care, as well as across the continuum of our healthcare and legal systems. That's a tall order!

Without effective physician leadership, transparency initiatives potentially will be designed and implemented inside healthcare that are not optimally oriented to patients and their physicians, or other providers who are delivering care. With that 30% waste and 10% error rate, pressures to improve our systems are inevitable. The ongoing pressure for increased transparency similarly will be assured.

Physician leadership is critical during these transitions to a better healthcare system.

Leadership is a lifelong learning process. In my opinion, the physician workforce is optimally placed to drive the processes for expanding the benefits of transparency in healthcare and to help further drive a true value-based system. A system that provides value to patients and organizations is highly efficient, safe and able to effectively demonstrate optimal quality of care in a transparent fashion.

Embrace the necessity for change and assume the leadership role you have the privilege of providing in our society as a physician. We look forward to how you will help clarify and further substantiate the critical importance of transparency in your own fashion. All of our patients and their families will benefit.

All physicians can be considered leaders. Creating a broader level of positive change in healthcare is within your capability.

CHAPTER 6

Redefining a Value Equation with Physicians as Leaders

Clarifying the value of physician leadership is essential. Redefining the value equation will be an eventual outcome.

Although physicians continue to provide, or directly supervise, almost 95% of patient care, they are not necessarily the pivot point around which healthcare is being redesigned or delivered for the future. The historical value of physicians and their leadership in healthcare is not guaranteed or assured.

Most of us know the value equation as Value = Quality/Cost But do we truly understand and fully appreciate the value of physician leadership?

Historically, healthcare revolved around the knowledge and decision-making of physicians. The Flexner Report and its related consequences from the early 1900s have now driven the orientation of healthcare education and clinical delivery strategies in profound fashion for more than 100 years. Being able to move beyond these legacy behaviors is recognized as complex, and it will take several more years before we can look back and note that significant change has occurred.

Also coming into play is the fact that our industry has several competing agendas gradually evolving. Shifting clinical delivery models, new financial payment models, multi-professional team-based care, changing continuing medical education platforms, and a continual flow of new policy initiatives are among the developments. Additionally, the non-physician clinical disciplines are evolving in their own approaches on how to contribute in new ways to patient care.

Paul Keckley, PhD, a renowned healthcare economist assisted me with a survey on clarifying the issues physician leaders face and how they achieve success. This includes the issues for physicians in informal leadership roles as well as those in titled positions.

Highlights of a recent AAPL member survey showed that 55% of respondents said they agreed or strongly agreed that the Affordable Care Act, passed in 2010, had "more good than bad" in it. In addition·

- 69% of respondents agreed or strongly agreed that physicians should be held accountable for costs of care in addition to quality of care.
- 57% of respondents agreed or strongly agreed that Accountable Care Organizations will be a permanent model for risk sharing with payers in years ahead.
- 63% of respondents disagreed or strongly disagreed that "the elimination of fee-for-service incentives in favor of value-based payments will hurt the quality of care provided patients."
- 58% of respondents agreed or strongly agreed that transparency about physicians' business dealings is a positive trend for the profession.

Also of interest is that a majority believe physician leaders are more likely to be able to improve physician satisfaction levels within the profession than non-physician leaders. More than half of the respondents identified physician leadership as being key to achieving success within their organizations.

Surveys and the data generated are imperfect research tools. Nonetheless, the information gleaned can provide insights on where to focus further research.

Corroborating the survey data by repeating the survey in other audiences also can provide improved understanding of the issues.

SEEKING VALUE

A broader approach toward value also is being developed around how to redefine the value equation for healthcare. There are numerous subcomponents for quality that require better definition and clarity. Creating improved quality has proved elusive for healthcare.

Managing price (or cost) is now recognized as one of the most poorly understood aspects of the healthcare industry. Transparency, microeconomics, macroeconomics and institutional financial or accounting strategies all contribute to this difficulty in managing the denominator of the value equation.

In the midst of this complexity, who is judging value? The patients? Physicians? Other providers? Health systems and hospitals?

Obviously, redefining value will take some time and involve a variety of vested parties.

Leadership, both formal and informal, is a lifelong learning process. In my opinion, the physician workforce is still optimally placed to help bridge the gap toward an improved, value-driven healthcare system. It's a system that will drive value to patients and organizations, one that is highly efficient, safe and with measurement that is able to effectively demonstrate optimal quality of care.

At some level, all physicians can be considered leaders. Creating a broader level of positive change in healthcare is within your capability. We look forward to how you will help clarify and substantiate the value of physician leadership in your pursuits.

CHAPTER 7

Adversity, Resilience, and Persistence

Physician leadership often has to deal with adversity, but resilience and balanced persistence can help ensure improved outcome—for you, other individuals, organizations, and society.

I enjoy endurance sports and spending time outdoors in difficult environments. I remember one day, for example, I was out running in the woods on muddy, puddle-laden trails in pouring rain. Part way through, I tripped, fell into a pool of murky water, and emerged completely covered in black ooze. After realizing I had no injury, I laughed at the situation for what I must have looked like and then carried on to complete what turned out to be a great run. I enjoyed it! This was not the first time I tripped on the trails, nor will it be the last. But why do I persist?

Certainly, I enjoy the physical benefits of lifelong fitness, but I also find that I relish that sense of accomplishment when something complex has been achieved. For me, it is often less about the journey and more about the result. Do not get me wrong here, though—although the results give me greater pleasure, the journey in these settings can also be deeply satisfying despite arduous and difficult circumstances.

Over time, I have benefited greatly by having my capabilities challenged by managing the difficulties of a journey and by learning to continually improve my approaches (mostly psychological). Those capabilities have improved because of my recognition that, when properly channeled, adversity inevitably will result in improved resilience. This, in turn, enables me with an improved ability to persist as I strive to reach my goals.

ADVERSITY

The *Merriam-Webster Dictionary* definition of adversity (noun) is: a difficult situation or condition; a misfortune or tragedy.

> "The most beautiful people we have known are those who have known defeat, known suffering, known struggle, known loss, and have found their way out of the depths. These persons have an appreciation, a sensitivity, and an understanding of life that fills them with compassion, gentleness, and a deep loving concern. Beautiful people do not just happen."

> — ELISABETH KÜBLER-ROSS
> Author. Well-recognized for
> 5 Stages of Grieving

Being physician leaders, we routinely face adversity—both professional and personal. We see numerous clinical examples daily, and we also see frequent examples of ways to manage it. The core nature of who we are as physicians, how we were trained and how we practice our skills helps provide us with the resilience to weather adversity.

RESILIENCE

The *Merriam-Webster Dictionary* definition of resilience (noun) is: able to become strong, healthy or successful again after something bad happens.

> "Resilient people do not let adversity define them. They find resilience by moving toward a goal beyond themselves, transcending pain and grief by perceiving bad times as a tem-

porary state of affairs . . . It's possible to strengthen your inner self and your belief in yourself, to define yourself as capable and competent. It's possible to fortify your psyche. It's possible to develop a sense of mastery."

— Hara Estroff Marano
Editor-at-Large for *Psychology Today*

Our long years of medical education require resilience! And then our persistence through that education prepares us to launch into a career trajectory that also requires ongoing resilience and persistence. Likely, most of us did not even recognize that we started to develop these critically important capabilities early in our careers. Turns out, it is a prescient set of skills.

As the healthcare industry continues to gain complexity and evolve at an ever-increasing pace, it is now almost imperative that if we do not already have natural resiliency, then we should each seek ways to gain it.

Almost all the adversities we witness in healthcare will continue in some fashion, and our need for persistence endures. Nonetheless, it is our personal resilience that will allow us to manage adversity better and use persistence to achieve better results.

PERSISTENCE

The *Merriam-Webster Dictionary* definition of persistence (noun) is: the quality that allows someone to continue doing something or trying to do something even though it is difficult or opposed by other people.

During World War II, well before my time, Winston Churchill tried to lift the spirits of the British people through an analogy for persistence. Knowing their ongoing fight with Germany was difficult, he painted the picture by saying, "The nose of the bulldog has been slanted backward so he can breathe without letting go (of his adversary)."

From what I understand, this was a well-accepted and highly motivational moment for the British public and the armed forces.

While writing this chapter, I also came across a clinically relevant article that provided deeper insight into the thinking of the International Society for Pharmacoeconomics and Outcomes Research Medication Compliance and Persistence Work Group—a group that developed clinical definitions for compliance and persistence during three years of international review and discussion.

"Clinical outcomes of treatment are affected not only by how well patients take their medications, but also by how long they take their medications. Thus, compliance and persistence should be defined and measured separately to characterize medication-taking behavior comprehensively. Addressing both compliance and persistence provides a richer understanding of medication-taking behavior."[1]

I found this latter nuance intriguing, and it has placed the simple act of patient engagement in a much clearer context for me, personally. Certainly, our patients require resilience for general health approaches and in all types of treatment strategies for illness.

For them, these represent adversity and they will each make personal choices on their eventual compliance with the recommended approaches. But, regardless, persistence is always needed because that is the nature of illness and disease — adverse situations usually do not just go away. Positive or negative results will prevail, depending on the success of the treatment.

As physician leaders, we have to continually develop these complex skills of resilience and persistence; not only as individuals, but also for our patients and the organizations in which we work. All physicians are viewed as leaders at some level, and often the presumption is that innately we already have the ability to manage adversity effectively.

That is not always the case and it underscores my point on the need for each of us to consider how to evaluate our existing degree of resilience and how to expand it. Our persistence in improving resilience will not only provide a better end result for our patients and our organizations, but also will benefit ourselves, our families and our circle of friends.

The story of Dr. Bennet Omalu is an intriguing story of exceptional success in taking on adversity with resilience and persistence. His early efforts in the past dozen years to define chronic traumatic encephalopathy in National Football League (NFL) players are continuing to be felt within professional sports around the globe.

In addition, there is now a recognition of potential head injuries within the general public, and this fact is dramatically changing the nature of organized amateur sports. For me, his story is not just about the NFL, but is one of scientific integrity that carries profound public health ramifications. By demonstrating personal resilience and effective persistence, Omalu overcame significant adversity to create a highly important end-result for society.

Physician leaders can learn a lot from stories about overcoming adversity. Physicians also can learn significantly from those highly motivated individuals we come across in the clinical delivery system—patients and providers.

We can all work toward creating large-scale change for healthcare by demonstrating resilience and persistence when it comes to improving the outcomes of patient care, and the outcomes for higher quality, safe, efficient systems of care. Our society benefits from the focus and skills of physicians when they serve as leaders. It is my core altruism and my personal commitment to physician leadership that helps drive me to improve my own resilience. I do this by seeking a variety of challenges, which represent adversity, and they help me grow through my persistence. So if you see a muddy-looking trail runner approach, please don't turn away—laugh with them and let them know you appreciate what is going on under their mud-covered clothing. I encourage you to find your own version of the muddy trails and enjoy what it brings to your ongoing personal growth.

REFERENCE

1. Cramer JA, Roy A, Burrell A, et al. Medication compliance and persistence: terminology and definitions. www.ispor.org/heor-resources/good-practices-for-outcomes-research/article/medication-compliance-and-persistence-terminology-and-definitions.

CHAPTER 8

Reflections on Evolving Change in the Training of Physicians

Physician leadership is increasingly recognized as pivotal for improved change in healthcare. Multi-professional care teams, education, and leadership are evolving trends that are important for healthcare's future.

I n spring of 2016, I was asked to make a presentation on the multi-professional aspects of healthcare. I found myself reflecting on a medical student experience that I had not pondered in many years—a premature obstetrical delivery that I became immersed in as a student without physician oversight. Fortunately, for the patient and myself, a seasoned nurse was present and helped me through the situation, and the patient and her baby did well.

Most of us have similar types of training stories. An unwritten rule during medical training has always been to make sure you get along well with the nurses; they will usually provide the proper direction when one is unsure. Other disciplines are also being recognized as similarly important for medical trainees (e.g., pharmacists, respiratory therapists, etc.). Clinical care has been functioning with this informal multi-professional team approach for quite some time.

Formalized, multi-professional clinical teams are now being developed and implemented in this country across several health systems and in numerous hospitals. They are becoming an expected norm in many settings, and their successes are profiled in workforce recruitment and marketing campaigns. Patients and families generally appreciate the team approaches and often have a stronger sense of confidence when a team is caring for a patient.

Interestingly, those same patients and families, however, still want the reassurance that their physician is involved and providing strong oversight or direction for the care. The physician role, therefore, remains a solid core within multi-professional team care. And as we know, 90% to 95% of clinical care is still directly provided by, or supervised by, physicians.

The clinical environment is changing, and we need to pay attention so that physicians as leaders (formal and informal) can help better shape that environment.

At the student training level within healthcare disciplines, we are still highly fragmented in terms of providing team-based education. Across the United States, there are only a few campuses where each of the clinical disciplines have training programs, and there usually isn't specific coordination of education. Likewise, the many simulation education centers are just beginning to create robust multi-professional team-training exercises. The expectation for trainees to leave their educational environments to function on patient care teams is unrealistic and perhaps naive. Yet this expectation persists in a majority of settings.

Fortunately, other efforts to establish multi-professional education are gathering momentum.

Most of the new medical schools getting started in the United States are incorporating these approaches at the very beginning of student training. The American Medical Association (AMA) initiated a well-received grant program for medical schools to develop and implement innovative curriculum strategies. The Accreditation Council for Graduate Medical Education has its Pursuing Excellence initiative, and the new National Coalition for Improving Clinical Learning Environments has also seen success.

Similarly, the National Academy of Medicine (formerly the Institute of Medicine) has an ongoing initiative for inter-professional education, defined by the World Health Organization as people from two or more professions learning with, from, and about each other to achieve better patient outcomes. The recognition of this trend clearly is important, and other initiatives will continue to emerge in the near future.

Years ago, the American Hospital Association and the AMA collaborated to release their "Integrated Leadership for Hospitals and Health Systems: Principles for Success." The six principles of success for integrated leadership between hospitals and physicians are:

1. **Physician and hospital leaders who are united:** Leadership should share similar values and expectations, and their financial and non-financial incentives should be aligned. Goals should be the same across the board, and responsibility should be shared for financial, cost, and quality targets. Leaders in both spheres should be jointly responsible for strategic planning, management, and engagement of patients as partners in care.

2. **An interdisciplinary structure that supports collaborative decision-making:** Physicians' clinical autonomy must be preserved to ensure quality patient care while they work with others to deliver effective, efficient, and appropriate care.

3. **Clinical physician and hospital leadership present at all levels of the health system:** All key management decisions should be made with representation from all clinicians, including nurses. Teams of clinicians and hospital or practice management administrators should lead together at every level of the health system, and should be accountable to, and for, each other.

4. **A partnership built on trust:** This sense of interdependence and working toward mutual achievement of the Triple Aim—better care, better health, and lower costs—is crucial to alignment be-

tween and engagement with physicians and hospital leaders. Those in clinical and hospital leadership positions also need to be able to trust each other's good faith and abilities.

5. **Open and transparent sharing of clinical and business information:** Sharing data with all parties across the health system can improve care.

6. **A clinical information system infrastructure that is useful:** The system should capture and report key clinical quality and efficiency performance data. Physicians and other clinicians should be involved in technology decisions that will affect their day-to-day practices.

Multi-professional care teams at the clinical delivery level, inter-professional education across healthcare disciplines, and integrated leadership approaches are rapidly coming to the forefront. These are evolving trends, but they are not fully coordinated, nor maturing at the same pace of adoption. Although the concepts are being recognized and developed sporadically, the likelihood of these trends disappearing is remote. Legislative, regulatory, and accreditation pressures will continue to build, and financial reform tactics will provide added pressure.

More often than not nowadays, when value is broached as the preferred end-result for healthcare, implicit in those considerations is some form of multi-professional team-based approach.

Fortunately, for the time being, physicians will remain as the predominant drivers of patient care. Although other clinical disciplines and non-clinical leaders have critically important roles that are evolving, the recognition of physicians as leaders in healthcare remains generally accepted across all aspects of the industry—including the policy and payer communities. Physicians need to embrace team-based care and must consider how their roles may evolve. How we as physicians help create these "new" systems of delivery is highly critical, from my perspective.

Since those days when I was an inexperienced, poorly supervised student, I have immensely enjoyed the benefits of teams. I certainly know that my patient's mother, her husband, and their family appreciated the benefits of a team behind that profusely sweating, doe-eyed and ill-prepared medical student so many years back. They not only appreciated it, they expected it, and our patients continue to deserve having well-performing teams providing care today.

Reflect further on your training stories. Reflect on how much you enjoyed working with the other disciplines. Remember the pride and joy of successful outcomes shared together. Remember the shared grief for less successful outcomes and how a mutually supportive team was able to move forward effectively. We all have these memories, not only from training days, but from our daily professional lives and our personal experiences. Team activities are rewarding and beneficial at so many levels and for so many reasons. Acknowledge the benefits of teams.

With all physicians being considered leaders, let us embrace the coming change toward multi-professional team-based care.

CHAPTER 9

Caring and Compassion vs. Physician Compensation

*Caring for people and compassion are core values for the vast major-
ity of physicians. Appropriately, the profession is held in high regard
by society, and for several decades, physicians have been hand-
somely rewarded financially. With healthcare a complex industry,
the increasing pressure on physician compensation and financial
models of payment certainly contribute to anxieties. Is there an
achievable balance in the evolving value-based compensation era
with physicians' core values?*

CARING FOR PEOPLE IS WHAT WE DO

Years ago, I was approached by someone in distress over a newly
made, poor-prognosis medical diagnosis. Yes, this happens
to each of us routinely. But what made me stop to reflect after
my discussion was the reflex reaction I had to feel empathy and to
show genuine concern for the person without considering any other
issues before engaging with her. It was an inherent response that, I
believe, always lies just under the emotional surface for each of us as
physicians.

Caring for people is a privilege and an honor we should continually
cherish. There are very few professions, or even other work environments, where people show up and expect to share their deepest
anxieties, troubles, and secrets. Physicians are trained to receive this

information in trusted confidence, and our patients usually want to use us this way. It is often a part of their healing—knowing that a caring person listened and demonstrated genuine concern.

In our perpetual quest to ferret out details on potential disease states in our patients, and to manage the excessive amount of related information, we should never forget this basic premise: We are basically here to care for people, and it is an instinctual drive for us as individuals that carries tremendous potential satisfaction in doing so effectively. Satisfaction for our patients . . . and ourselves.

COMPASSION

At about the same time I was approached by the person mentioned, I also had the opportunity to attend a conference related to the well-being of physicians. It was co-sponsored by the American Medical Association, British Medical Association, and Canadian Medical Association, a relatively new annual meeting called the International Conference on Physician Health. That year's theme: increasing joy in medicine.

We are all aware of the concern on morale within the physician workforce (including trainees). It's likely there was some implicit bias among the attendees, but an overwhelming undertone I consistently detected throughout the conference was the compassion physicians continue to have for their patients, knowing the critically important role physicians have in patients' lives. At every session and in each discussion forum, there always was a comment of some type related to compassion.

It was easy to recognize the high levels of compassion for patients and the desire to remain as compassionate caregivers. This recognition was important for all attendees but also important for me personally. I have been away from direct patient care many years now but remain highly engaged with safety and quality initiatives. Appreciating once

again the drive that most physicians carry toward being compassionate caregivers further affirms my drive for the important work we are
moving forward on within the association—helping all physicians
become better leaders.

So how do we ensure we don't lose our core value of compassion,
and actually better leverage it?

An important concept still being delineated in a variety of social
sciences is that of self-compassion. To some degree, it is that old
mantra of looking after yourself so you can look after others better.
And yet it is more than simply eating well, getting plenty of exercise,
and obtaining good sleep. There is an emerging recognition that
treating ourselves kindly and compassionately (emotionally and
psychologically), as we would treat a patient, can be vitally important
to our general well-being and sense of happiness. This translates to a
more-positive approach to our daily lives and to improved interactions
with others—especially patients and our families.

ALTERNATIVE PAYMENT MODELS

How will the evolving payment system create compassion and improve
our caring for people?

There is no simple answer to that question. There is, however, an
important recognition for us all—value-based payment methodologies
are here for the foreseeable future. Unfortunately, there are several
tests and experimental models that will be present for the next few
years. We cannot predict the future, but we can know the direction
it's headed.

In November 2016, the Department of Health and Human Services
(HHS) finalized its policy implementing the Merit-Based Incentive
Payment System and the Advanced Alternative Payment Models
incentive payment provisions in the Medicare Access and CHIP
Reauthorization Act of 2015 (aka MACRA). Collectively, it's called
the Quality Payment Program.

According to HHS, the Quality Payment Program gradually will transform Medicare payments for more than 600,000 clinicians across the country. HHS considers it a major step in improving care across the entire healthcare system. The Quality Payment Program, which replaces the flawed Sustainable Growth Rate, is designed to give clinicians the tools and flexibility to provide high-quality, patient-centered care.

Further, this initiative offers a fresh start for Medicare by focusing payments around the care that is best for the patients, providing more options to clinicians for innovative care and payment approaches, and reducing administrative burden to give clinicians more time to spend with their patients, instead of on paperwork. With clinicians as partners, HHS built a system that delivers better care—one in which clinicians work together and fully understand patients' needs, Medicare pays for what works and spends taxpayer money more wisely, and patients are in the center of their care. The result: a healthier country.

COMPENSATION

There are a variety of groups delivering benchmark surveys of physician compensation. These are important sources of information, and physicians should review them on an annual or bi-annual basis. It is important to know the market value of your discipline, because it helps you negotiate fair compensation arrangements.

Being psychologically assured your compensation is at, or near, market value certainly contributes to a better sense of self-worth and personal happiness. If you are not near market value, then it is also good to know that information for negotiation purposes.

THE BALANCE

Balancing core values with fair financial reward is a complex affair, especially when the external influences on both seem to be beyond our personal control and our ability to influence outcomes directly.

Learning to look after ourselves with a certain degree of self-compassion will help—mainly by contributing to a calmer and happier disposition. Focusing on our patients by drawing on our core values, such as caring for people and our inherent compassion, also will contribute to a better balance. Keeping up with evolving trends and learning how to anticipate them, even though you cannot control them, helps you manage change. And knowing your value in the marketplace helps you ensure appropriate reward for the kind, caring quality you and your team provide patients.

By the way, the person who approached me with a poor prognosis had followed an expected clinical course and did not live past the calendar year. Before she passed, she wrote me a thank-you note that brought tears to my eyes. In it, she mentioned how often she reflected on the kind, caring words of advice I provided in her moment of need. Apparently, my words continued to give her strength and courage as she received treatment for a hopeless situation. Her words to me are more than enough compensation.

Regardless of your career stage or chronological age, it is important to reflect routinely on your core values—caring for people and compassion being only two. In this reflection, there also is opportunity to reframe the value that you contribute to your environment. What is your value-based contribution to your patients and to yourself? It is not just about the money, but you should be at fair-market value.

Helping manage industry transitions proactively is a critical component of our professional responsibility and has been since our beginnings.

CHAPTER 10

Metrics, Measurement, and Patient Safety Reporting

*Healthcare, like most all other industries, has clearly entered an
era where measurement and reporting have increasing importance.*

A t its most basic, our clinical care practices have an historical
basis on research and education—both of which rely on
metrics, measurement, unbiased evaluation, and reporting.
Unfortunately, the science for measurement of clinical care practices,
and related outcomes, continues to be relatively immature. The sub-
sequent reporting, therefore, is often inexact.

Physicians are well recognized as a professional group where data
is highly valued, and the integrity of that data is considered to be pivotal for decision-making. In fact, this expectation by physicians for
quality data is often recognized to filter into their decision-making
for non-clinical situations as well. Subsequently, when data for any
given situation becomes suspect from physicians' vantage points, the
outputs generated from that data are usually suspect as well.

For clinical situations, learning how to obtain good outcomes when
having to make care decisions with incomplete or flawed data becomes
part of the "art" in medicine. Fortunately, the vast majority of physicians are able to refine this art successfully. Finding that balance in
the non-clinical arena, however, can become even more challenging
and occasionally frustrating for many physicians.

The National Quality Forum (NQF) developed and published an excellent report in February 2011 regarding consensus standards for public reporting of safety data.[1] In participating with the development of this report, I came to appreciate the importance for the following guiding principles of public reporting:

1. Entities that provide public reports of patient safety information are accountable for the quality of the reports they produce, including the timeliness and accuracy of information and the relevance and usefulness of the information to the decision-making of consumers.

2. Public reports of patient safety event information should heighten collective public awareness and concern about safety in a way that stimulates providers, healthcare organizations, and entities responsible for setting public policy to make improvements.

3. Publicly reported information about patient safety events must be previewed for accuracy by those about whom it is reported, corrected as necessary, and then displayed in ways that facilitate appropriate and informed decision-making by consumers.

4. To facilitate understanding and accountability, public reporters must use tested tools to properly convey information about the wide array of event characteristics, including those that occur frequently and those that occur rarely or with low frequency.

5. The accuracy and completeness of information in public reports should be verifiable through means such as audits, crosschecks with multiple data sources, attestations by reporting organizations, and/or other means.

6. Because the science that underpins public reporting is evolving, it is important that public reports are continually assessed for usefulness and validity and revised as the science improves.

7. To advance improvements in understanding and improving patient safety, it is essential to bring uniformity to definitions,

patient safety measurement tools, and approaches to analysis and classification of events.

8. Information in public reports should be presented in a way that increases consumers' awareness and understanding of patient safety events, including preventability, by providing context, explanations, and information about their role in improving patient safety for themselves and others.

9. Consumer involvement in the development of patient safety public reports is particularly important because of the significance of the information and its propensity to be highly technical in both terms and definitions.

10. Translating this information into useful, actionable tools requires the active involvement of consumers in report construction. Patient confidentiality must be maintained.

11. Complete transparency of methodology and sources should be required for all measures included in public reports.

The guiding principles listed from this NQF report work together as an interconnected set. While much of this information is focused on safety events, I believe the collective set provides important guidance for metrics, measurement and reporting in general. I strongly encourage increased adoption of these guiding principles. In this process, physician leaders should also endeavor to become more aware of the constellation of measurement and reporting initiatives that continue to crop-up and evolve around the country; as well as in other countries. They are here to stay!

From my perspective, the good news is that this type of measurement and reporting in healthcare is evolving rapidly and that in recent years the quality of the science behind measurement has garnered increased support on many levels. All industries need metrics, measurement, and reporting in order to improve.

REFERENCE

1. National Voluntary Consensus Standards for Public Reporting of Patient Safety Event Information: A Consensus Report. National Quality Forum. Washington, DC; 2010. http://www.qualityforum.org/Publications/2011/02/National_Voluntary_Consensus_ Standards_for_Public_Reporting_of_Patient_Safety_Event_Information.aspx.

CHAPTER 11

Diversity, Inclusion, and Physicians' Need to Give

Diversity and inclusion finally are being addressed within academia, corporations, governments, and general society. There are numerous issues and nuances within diversity, and the path forward is far from complete. Progress and change are critical for success.

I happened to be attending a December meeting in Manhattan on the same day as the state funeral of President George H.W. Bush in Washington, DC. New York was full of the pre-holiday joy and busyness that so many people from round the world come to seek as a rite of passage. In contrast, the ceremony for President Bush was equally global in its breadth of representation, but clearly much more somber in its purpose and intent. Both, however, created reflection on our global diversity and our ongoing needs to be more inclusive with one another as human beings.

Most of us recognize more women have been entering medical school for many years now, and the data is starting to show positive change. In 2009, the Liaison Committee on Medical Education (LCME), for one, introduced two diversity accreditation standards, mandating U.S. allopathic medical schools to engage in systematic efforts to attract and retain students from diverse backgrounds.

In a letter to *JAMA*, Dowin Boatright, MD, of Yale School of Medicine and lead researcher of a recent study on the effect of this LCME program, notes:

"From 2002 to 2009, before the standards were introduced, the proportion of women entering medical school was decreasing by 0.29 percent a year. That changed to an increase of 0.85 percent from 2012 to 2017. For African Americans, the proportions went from an annual decrease of 0.09 percent to an increase of 0.27 percent over the same time periods. Hispanic matriculation was already increasing by 0.18 percent a year in the earlier period, and almost doubled to 0.35 percent."[1]

And while there are more than 980,000 licensed U.S. physicians, according to the Federation of State Medical Boards, 30.3% of physicians are now over 60 years of age, and roughly two-thirds are male.[2] But the number of female licensed physicians has been increasing annually for the past several years.

Clearly, shifts are occurring in our professional demographics, and we all need to be prepared to accommodate these ongoing changes. So how, as leaders, do we proactively address these shifts? In his report, "What Makes a School Multicultural?,"[3] Eastern University sociologist Caleb Rosado, who specializes in diversity and multiculturalism, identifies seven important actions involved in defining multiculturalism:

- Recognizing the abundant diversity of cultures;
- Respecting the differences;
- Acknowledging the validity of different cultural expressions and contributions;
- Valuing what other cultures offer;
- Encouraging the contribution of diverse groups;
- Empowering people to strengthen themselves and others to achieve their maximum potential by being critical of their own biases; and
- Celebrating rather than just tolerating the differences in order to bring about unity through diversity.

As you consider your own personal and leadership efforts in this regard, and how best to incorporate change, here are a couple of definitions from Diversity.com to help in your reflections:

What is diversity? The short answer for the question is: "diversity and inclusive practice includes gender, religious, race, age, disability, linguistic differences, socio-economic status and cultural background."

What is inclusion? Likewise, a brief answer is: "Inclusive practice is known to be attitudes, approaches and strategies taken to make sure that students are not excluded from the learning environment because of their differences."

Giving of oneself, for me, is a core philosophy by which I recognize the ongoing need to keep giving of myself, so that I can best shift my own attitudes and approaches with others. I do this to continue improving and incorporating internal changes, to become even more inclusive of diversity in all its forms and formats. Hopefully, I keep growing as a result. This is a never-ending process of change; I encourage each of you to also move along this particular path of perpetual learning and maturing as leaders in your own organization and within your personal lives.

Thomas Nasca, MD, from the Accreditation Council for Graduate Medical Education, once told Georgetown University School of Medicine graduates, "Every patient has a 'why.' We need to listen. We need to hear it, so we can help them with the 'how,' so that they can achieve it. Your soul will be enriched by each person you care for. Pursue your calling with vigor, with commitment, with kindness, and, whenever in doubt, remember the 'why' that's in your hearts today."[4] It's a powerful message, recognizing the importance of giving that is as true for each of us promulgating leadership as it is for fresh physician graduates.

Giving of oneself also can be viewed as an uncommon form of gifting to others. While giving and gifting is too detailed a topic to cover here, Lewis Hyde's book *The Gift* provides a twist on the concept of gifts and giving of ourselves.[5] He writes, "It is also the case that a gift may be the actual agent of change, the bearer of new life." He talks about how the gifts within ourselves are also awakened when we experience the work of others and how they are shared. He further notes " . . . it is essential gifts are shared and kept moving within a community. This leads to increased connectivity and relationships, and transformative inspiration."

For those who might be intrigued, since Marcel Mauss' influential book *Essai sur le Don* first appeared in 1925,[6] the primary work on giving and gift exchange apparently has been within anthropology as it relates to giving among or between groups of individuals. Medical sociologists only recently have begun to emerge in their considerations of gift-giving—earlier work being done by Richard Titmuss in 1970, when he published *The Gift Relationship*, a study on how we handle human blood for transfusion.[7] For example, the British system classifies all blood as a gift, whereas the U.S. system has a mixed economy in which some blood is donated, and some is bought and sold.

An interesting side thought, perhaps: Within our scientific communities, gifts also can be viewed as coming in the form of scientific presentations, intellectual articles and the sharing of theories within various communities. Therefore, the sciences arguably already have advanced rapidly in giving and gifting—increasing our connectivity and our communities.

At their core, physicians are compassionate, giving people who care deeply about others and give of ourselves routinely. Let your own altruism continue to surface so that all those around you are aware of the giving you provide with your gifts to humanity. It is what we do—it is our calling to help and care for others that ultimately benefits society. Accept the gifts of others in the process so that you are able to remain healthy and better balanced in your own approaches within this complex profession.

Atul Gawande, MD, a prominent surgeon in the Harvard system and CEO of the healthcare venture formed by Amazon, Berkshire Hathaway, and JPMorgan Chase, said in a 2004 commencement speech: "The life of a doctor is an intense life. We are witnesses and servants to individual human survival. The difficulty is that we are also only humans ourselves. We cannot live simply for patients. In the end, we must live our own lives."[8]

We must live our own lives in a healthier, more-balanced fashion to minimize the untoward effects of this demanding profession. Giving of ourselves, while honorable and uplifting, can be draining at times. As Hyde suggests, a gift from others may be the actual agent of change, the bearer of new life. It is therefore acceptable to not only give, but to also receive.

I encourage each of us to continue seeking deeper levels for how we can become more inclusive of the diversity in our evolving society. We can generate positive influence in this at all levels.

REFERENCES:

1. https://www.nbcnews.com/health/health-news/diversity-standards-produce-more-women-minorities-med-school-n943731
2. Young A, Chaudhry HJ, Pei X, et al. FSMB Census of Licensed Physicians in the United States, 2018. Journal of Medical Regulation. 2019;105(2);7-23. www.fsmb.org/siteassets/advocacy/publications/2018census.pdf.
3. https://red.pucp.edu.pe/ridei/files/2012/11/121116.pdf
4. https://gumc.georgetown.edu/gumc-stories/school-of-medicine-celebrates-166th-graduating-class/
5. Hyde L. *The Gift.* New York: Random House. 2007.
6. Mauss M. Essai sur le Don.1925.
7. Titmuss R. The Gift Relationship. 1970.
8. https://bulletin.facs.org/2018/12/presidential-address-for-our-patients/

CHAPTER 12

The Value of Volunteering

Volunteering provides valuable service to society and a great amount of satisfaction for the physician volunteer.

Volunteerism is the policy or practice of giving time or talents for charitable, educational, or other worthwhile activities, especially in your community. By definition, volunteering is an altruistic activity intended to promote goodness or improve quality of life. In return, this activity can produce a feeling of self-worth and respect. There is no financial gain involved for the individual. Volunteering is also known for skill development, socialization and fun.

Skills-based volunteering is leveraging the specialized skills and talents of individuals to strengthen the infrastructure of nonprofits, helping them build and sustain their capacity to successfully achieve their missions. Many volunteers are specifically trained in the areas in which they work, such as medicine or education. Others serve on an as needed basis, such as in response to a natural disaster.

Several of us were brought up in environments in which volunteering was a routine part of life; while for others, volunteering is a learned activity. Either way, the benefits are easily recognized. When you engage, it can help clarify who you are and consolidate your personal values as you contribute for the benefit of others.

You can volunteer in a health system or professional society, or you can volunteer to help with a variety of community services—local, regional, national, or international. Some would say both types of volunteerism are equal in importance, while others would make a distinction. I believe any type of volunteering holds value.

"A noble leader answers not to the trumpet calls of self-promotion, but to the hushed whispers of necessity."

— MOLLIE MARTI

"The interior joy we feel when we have done a good deed is the nourishment the soul requires. Wherever you turn, you can find someone who needs you. Even if it is a little thing, do something for which there is no pay but the privilege of doing it. Remember, you do not live in a world all of your own."

— ALBERT SCHWEITZER

When you are providing a contribution to a worthwhile endeavor, there are benefits for you as well as those you are helping. The value achieved does not need to have quantifiable parameters and should not necessarily require objective assessments from disengaged external reviewers.

I do agree, however, that there needs to be some form of data (qualitative and quantitative) available to help volunteers decide when, where, or how they can provide meaningful volunteer work. I also believe that only providing a financial contribution is not truly volunteerism. Certainly, financial contributions help create important and significant change in our society. But active participation in volunteerism means making an impact yourself and observing true change.

So what does volunteerism actually entail for a healthcare professional? This is a complex question to answer.

Traditional approaches include participating on committees, helping to develop educational courses, and engaging with thought leadership initiatives. These are all still important. Many pursue these for academic advancement, while others desire to contribute back to benefit the organization from an altruistic perspective. At the end of the day, however, both are equally important, and it is critical to recognize that a sense of community is often the primary motivating factor for everyone.

It is also engaging to learn from others when it comes to volunteerism. There are fascinating stories to share and opportunities to learn about new initiatives. Often, there is a fresh type of activity that one would never have considered if not through the simple act of sharing. Sharing and engaging with each other is where a sense of community can arise and flourish.

Is volunteering valuable? The answer is a simple "yes." Participate in what is meaningful for you and use the skills that you are best able to provide. The benefits are mutual for the receiver and the provider. Try it; you'll like it.

At some level, all physicians can be considered leaders. And leaders often give back to our society when an opportunity is available.

CHAPTER 13

Violence, Safety, and Physician Leadership

Ensuring healthcare worker safety is more complicated than simple security, but physician leadership can help it become reality.

B ack in November 2015, a murder-suicide happened inside one of our local hospitals in the Tampa Bay area. The victims were visiting an ill relative, and no healthcare workers were involved. The local media covered the event extensively and questioned all sorts of issues related to security and protection.

Not surprisingly, several of our staff members became quite concerned about how this could happen and why this could even be possible. The event was very real for everyone.

Then the Paris Bataclan terrorist killings occurred, followed quickly by the San Bernardino rampage. In the background were growing concerns about increasing gun violence and murder rates in our cities, other mass shootings, and incidents of police violence against citizens. All of this feeds the political rhetoric that dominates the news media.

The United States is not alone in this either—many countries experienced, and continue to grapple with, similar concerns.

Closer to home, management of our office building had mandated that all organizations and companies provide a video review to their staff about a "shooter-on-the-prowl" scenario, encouraging each company to practice its reactions. We complied but did not have full context for why this was necessary. We were safe—right?

For me, this increased awareness of societal violence is an issue I had not recently considered deeply on a personal level. I had become complacent in my view of how much impact these events can create in our everyday worlds. That complacency bothered me.

Coming from an academic clinical background of trauma surgery and surgical critical care, I have been intimately involved with managing critically ill patients, operating on the injured, and watching far too many victims die. Historically, I also participated in a wide range of violence prevention initiatives and still continue following the medical literature related to violence prevention. There was indeed a time when I cared passionately about these issues and had sought to create change.

WHEN AND WHY DID MY COMPLACENCY SET IN?

I am not the only one who has developed a degree of complacency for societal violence. Acts of violence are increasing, and the media coverage is expanding. Gradually, a different norm is being established in terms of how we collectively assimilate acts of violence into our expectations of society. Many of us are now more complacent and inured to the violence happening around us. Our children just view it all as an expected aspect of life, unfortunately.

Sure, we expect our societal values to change with each generation. But this complacency toward violence and purposeful harm toward others is one that broaches unethical behavior. I personally need to rekindle my own awareness of violence and work to prevent it. I believe that, as physician leaders, each of us needs to help provide focus on workplace safety.

I remember all too well the mass casualty drills I participated in as a trauma surgeon. The drills sometimes didn't go well. But then when significant events did occur, often the various teams pulled together in remarkable ways to provide excellent triage and care.

Relying on "swarm intelligence," a term coined by physicians who helped analyze responses to the Boston Marathon bombing, is not enough, however. At the very least, we, as leaders in our profession, should look critically at our workplace environments in order to reevaluate the safety and efficacy of our violence-prevention programs. Consider how to prevent a violent act from occurring and how to safely manage an event if one occurs. These safety efforts often start with a strong Failure Modes and Effects Analysis.[1] If you have not done one, it's worth considering.

COMMUNITY RESPONSE

But as physician leaders, our vigilance should potentially extend beyond our workplaces to our communities. Medical professionals are considered leaders in society. When bad events happen in a community, there is an unspoken expectation that the physicians and other medical professionals will mobilize and support the community.

Is there something you can do to help prevent violence in your community?

Creating large-scale change in public health requires commitment, resources and a great amount of time. Our anti-smoking efforts and motor vehicle safety initiatives took decades to reach their current levels of improvement. Other public health initiatives are only in their infancy and struggle along. Violence prevention is lagging, unfortunately.

Teams of professionals dedicated to public health certainly deserve credit and reward for their long-term vision and perseverance as they work to create societal change. Physician leaders can learn a lot from them. Highly motivated individuals also can generate energy toward creating large-scale change. If you have the opportunity, it is always enlightening to spend time with a highly motivated individual and take a lesson from his or her playbook for how to create societal change.

Physician leadership is critical to curbing violence in health systems and the greater community. Join me in losing complacency toward violence. Embrace the necessity for change as our societal norms shift and assume the leadership role you have the privilege of holding in our society as a physician. All of our patients and their families will be safer, as will our fellow healthcare workers.

REFERENCE

1. http://www.ihi.org/resources/Pages/Tools/FailureModesandEffectsAnalysisTool.aspx

CHAPTER 14

Clarion Call: Elective, Urgent, or Emergent?

The need for increased attention on dwindling healthcare workforce morale and professional satisfaction is more pressing than ever. Awareness of its incidence and prevalence is expanding, and each of us must decide how important it is individually. As many of our peers struggle, it's our duty to respond and assist as we're best able—and this includes using our association's resources.

Without barraging us all with an excess dismal statistics, I will simply state that worrisome data on physician workforce morale has accrued rapidly the past few years. For example, in the Medscape National Physician Burnout & Suicide Report 2020: The Generational Divide, more than 15,000 physicians surveyed identified four concerns as the leading causes of burnout: too many bureaucratic tasks, spending too many hours at work, feeling like just a cog in a wheel, and the increased computerization of practice.[1] Physicians from 29 specialties graded the severity of their burnout. The Medscape survey results rank burnout by specialty based on feedback from 15,000 physicians:

1. Urology >54%
2. Neurology >50%
3. Nephrology >49%
4. Diabetes/Endocrinology >46%
5. Radiology >46%
6. Family medicine >46%

7. Obstetrics/Gynecology >46%
8. Rheumatology >46%
9. Infectious disease >45%
10. Internal medicine >44%
11. Critical care >44%
12. Cardiology >44%
13. Emergency medicine >43%
14. Physical Medicine/Rehabilitation >43%
15. Oncology >42%
16. Pediatrics >41%
17. Anesthesiology >41%
18. Pulmonary medicine >41%
19. Allergy and Immunology >38%
20. Plastic Surgery >37%
21. Gastroenterology >36%
22. Pathology >36%
23. Dermatology >36%
24. Otolaryngology >35%
25. General surgery >35%
26. Psychiatry/Mental Health >35%
27. Orthopedics >34%
28. Ophthalmology >30%
29. Public Health and Preventive Medicine >29%

Numerous influence groups within healthcare have recognized similar trends and are calling for action. Several professional discipline organizations also have begun rolling out a host of offerings related to symptom relief, such as providing insights oriented to resilience training or how to develop a mindfulness practice. The clarion call is loud, and its focus is progressively sharpening.

Regardless of your own personal sense of discomfort, the data clearly shows that all levels of the physician workforce are being affected to some degree and with high incidence rates—from students to the most-seasoned practitioners.[2] Even if we don't personally feel it, we certainly all know someone who is feeling the burden of our industry's current complexity and is not necessarily able to live a happy, positive life.

These sets of issues fill the spectrum: from "not a problem, thanks" to "maybe I will check into it further someday" (elective) to "I recognize how it is effecting my performance" (urgent) to "I damn well better get something sorted out quick or it will all unravel on me further" (emergent). And we're all affected.

Interestingly, "burnout" is not recognized as a distinct disorder in the *Diagnostic and Statistical Manual of Mental Disorders, 5th edition.* However, it is included in the *International Classification of Diseases, Tenth Revision* (ICD-10)—not as a disorder, but under problems related to life-management difficulty. As I try to better understand the issues, it seems the view of burnout as a form of depression is finding common support.[3]

Fun fact: The phrase "burnt out" was part of the title of a Graham Greene novel, *A Burnt-Out Case*, about a doctor working in the Belgian Congo with leprosy patients. And so the term likely originated within healthcare and subsequently gained widespread popularity outside its generalized use in psychology research.

WE'RE NOT ALONE

To be sure, physicians are not the only individuals struggling with predilections for burnout or less-than-optimal job satisfaction. We all know that nursing is aware of this problem, as are several other clinical and ancillary healthcare professions. As well, outside our industry, there are numerous other professions or job types (e.g., dentistry, law enforcement, factory workers, etc.) with similar issues.

While individuals might find ways to cope with symptoms of burnout (e.g., resilience training and mindfulness), to truly prevent burnout there needs to be a combination of organizational (systems) change and awareness building (education) for individuals.

Maslach and Leiter postulated that burnout occurs when there is a disconnect between the organization and the individual regarding what they called the six areas of work-life: workload, control, reward, community, fairness, and values.[4] Resolving these discrepancies requires integrated action on the part of both the individual and the organization. A better connection on workload means assuring adequate resources to meet demands as well as work-life balances that encourage employees to revitalize their energy. A better connection on values means clear organizational values to which employees can feel committed. A better connection on community means supportive leadership and relationships with colleagues rather than discord.

But let's be clear: Not everyone is burned out, nor even on the cusp of being dissatisfied with their profession. Most physicians remain happy with their choice of becoming a physician, and many continue to practice in environments that provide them deep levels of professional satisfaction. Let us not forget about these fine individuals who continue to excel while others struggle. We all have things to learn from these peers that can become transferrable skills and learned approaches on a broader level.

And such is the case as well for non-physician providers—we are not in this alone. It's just a reality that the adverse physician statistics are higher than with other providers and the general population.

SHARING STORIES

Those who listen to National Public Radio often enjoy Friday mornings because that's when the StoryCorps features air. StoryCorps is an independent, nonprofit project that celebrates the lives of everyday Americans by sharing their stories. A recent piece caught my attention during a commute as I was thinking about the sets of issues hitting the morale of our workforce.[5]

For 25 years, the Rev. Noel Hickie, 74, and Marcia Hilton, 70, helped families during their most trying moments. Hickie was working as a hospital chaplain and Hilton as a bereavement counselor when the two met at a hospital in Eugene, Oregon. As I listened to the segment about their work (available at storycorps.org), tears welled up and I needed to pull over from my drive for a few moments.

During my clinically active years with trauma surgery and surgical critical care, I participated in far too many end-of-life decisions and a host of individual discussions projecting the lifestyle effects of newly acquired complex disabilities. Hickie and Hilton describe caring similarly for others and how their own lives were affected, and how they both carried on in this vein for so many years because of their deep belief in the importance of helping others in difficult life situations—not for themselves as providers, but for the people affected.

I resonated with the scenarios they described, and also immediately felt a sense of deep pride in knowing that many incredibly strong individuals in our various fields continue to create highly significant impacts on others' lives through this kind of work, and how so many are able to do so because of their intense commitments and beliefs in helping others. Fortunately for us all, numerous physicians— and non-physicians such as Hickie and Hilton—are able to find, or keep their balance with, the six key areas of workload, control, reward, community, fairness, and values.

ANSWERING THE CALL

As physicians, we must continually seek out the uncertainty in our own lives and optimize our personal situations. Personal insight and increased awareness are essential steps for achieving improved leadership—not only for the individuals and organizations we influence, but additionally for ourselves as humans.

I encourage all of us to continue seeking deeper levels of understanding for ourselves. Proactively helping others (including our peers) to better manage their life transitions is a critical component of our professional responsibility—in fact, it has been a professional responsibility since our beginnings.

REFERENCES

1. Medscape National Physician Burnout & Suicide Report 2020: The Generational Divide, https://www.medscape.com/slideshow/2020-lifestyle-burnout-6012460?src=WNL_physrep_200115_burnout2020&uac=287507PN&impID=2245458&faf=1#1

2. Shanafelt TD, West CP, Sinsky C, et al. Changes in burnout and satisfaction with work-life integration in physicians and the general US working population between 2011 and 2017. *Mayo Clinic Proceedings.* 2019;94:1681-1604. https://www.mayoclinicproceedings.org/article/S0025-6196(18)30938-8/fulltext.

3. https://www.cdc.gov/nchs/icd/data/10cmguidelines-FY2019-final.pdf

4. Maslach C, Schaufeli WB, Leiter MP. Job burnout. *Annual Review of Psychology.* 2001;52: 97–422. 97

5. https://www.npr.org/2017/07/28/539726037/for-decades-these-caregivers-helped-patients-families-through-illness-and-death

CHAPTER 15

Uncertainty, Ambiguity, and DiSC®: A Contrast

We often dramatically change patients' lives by creating medical uncertainty and unintentional ambiguity. This is because how messages are delivered and received depends on preset expectations. As physicians, we have expectations for our careers, and how we choose to manage them often will determine our satisfaction. Uncertainty and ambiguity are unwanted.

They got the call just after midnight. Halfway across the country, their adult son had been ejected from a moving vehicle at high speed and was being transferred to the regional trauma center with a head injury and multiple fractures. He already was intubated, chemically paralyzed, and sedated. Immediately, their world had become uncertain, and the early messages being received were full of ambiguous commentary. Their sense that normalcy was no longer was apparent.

As physicians, regardless of our chosen discipline, we frequently embroil ourselves in our patients' lives as they learn about fresh medical uncertainty arriving unwanted. We often are the ones delivering these messages. And, unfortunately, all too often in our busyness, we occasionally forget just how deep an impact we create on people's lives—especially if we have not considered their immediate sense of uncertainty and how our own unintended delivery of ambiguous messages may contribute to it.

We need to be ever mindful that we all—patients and physicians—often carry preset expectations for how these interactions will occur when delivering or receiving difficult messages. The public media representation on healthcare delivery practices, and the stereotypes portrayed, can be a disservice to our industry at times. All too frequently, the harshness of human behavior is highlighted in both patients and care providers. Occasionally, however, the genuineness of how clinical providers interact with patients and families is more accurately rendered. These portrayals beautifully demonstrate the empathy and altruism that drive so many of us, and they also can give us personal reassurance that we are indeed privileged to be in an honorable profession.

That these portrayals also make for good "production" further emphasizes how we as humans are inherently drawn to emotionally charged situations. It is built within us all to react with genuine emotion to the complex situations of others, and for how we might help others caught in those situations. Physicians, in particular, do this well, but so do most other healthcare providers.

These stereotypes are but one example of how our preset expectations arise—for patients and for care providers. Others come from our parents, our families, our culture, our readings, and our peers.

HEALTHCARE IS UNCERTAIN AND AMBIGUOUS

Our industry continues to remain complex, and it will be for generations to come. At its essence, U.S. healthcare is still a free-market economy. There are numerous sectors inside the industry, including federal and state governments, that create influence of varying degree. As each sector attempts to assert its importance, pressure is exerted on the industry that may or may not have demonstrable impact. This ongoing plethora of influences is considered a positive element for any type of free market.

This plethora, however, also creates a routine, constant element of uncertainty and ambiguity for those involved in the industry.

How so? Specifically, the difficulty comes in trying to decide how or when to predict which influence (or set of influences) will create the most significant impact(s) that should be followed as an established trend that ultimately improves (or harms) industry practices.

Physicians have been focused primarily on the quickly changing trends in clinical care for several decades. We all know the rapid dissemination of medical knowledge is difficult to keep pace with, and evolving technologies make this even more complicated. Which trends in clinical care, in addition to measurement and reporting of clinical outcomes, are most relevant? Often, that's too difficult an answer to generate. The creep of uncertainty and ambiguity starts even in our cherished clinical arenas.

There are numerous studies demonstrating the dwindling morale within the physician workforce. While most physicians are happy with their career choice, the morale problems come primarily from a host of nonclinical issues and influences. Electronic health records, increased bureaucracy and overhead, dwindling compensation despite increased work hours—the list goes on, each independently and collectively compounding the sense of uncertainty and ambiguity.

The stereotype of what the profession is supposed to deliver for physicians and their lifestyles continues to change routinely. Our expectations, therefore, also must change routinely. And we all know changing expectations—after so many years of education, training and practice development—can be exceedingly difficult. However, there is some evidence out there we are indeed changing, albeit gradually. One example is the trend toward employment.

IS DiSC® AN INFLUENCE?

Inherently, most physicians do not enjoy uncertainty and ambiguity. Yes, we are human, but physicians also develop certain attributes that

---

DiSC® PROFILE

Dominance: Person places emphasis on accomplishing results, the bottom line, confidence:
- Sees the big picture
- Can be blunt
- Accepts challenges
- Gets straight to the point

Influence: Person places emphasis on influencing or persuading others, openness, relationships:
- Shows enthusiasm
- Is optimistic
- Likes to collaborate
- Dislikes being ignored

Steadiness: Person places emphasis on cooperation, sincerity, dependability:
- Doesn't like to be rushed
- Calm manner
- Calm approach
- Supportive actions

Conscientiousness: Person places emphasis on quality and accuracy, expertise, competency
- Enjoys independence
- Objective reasoning
- Wants the details
- Fears being wrong

---

can make accepting change even more difficult. Learning about these can help each of us deal with change better.

Psychometric profile development can be useful in several ways, and I routinely encourage people to embrace what they represent. One tool—the DiSC® profile—is used quite frequently.[1] Each letter represents a personality type within the workforce, of which there are four types (see sidebar).

Overall, physicians tend to be quite high in the controlling characteristics related to dominance, and also fairly high in those related to conscientiousness—so much so, that I have coined a term: We tend to be a bunch of "conscientious dominators" in our professional and daily lives.

Together, these two attributes alone make us want to be in control and to control the details of the situations within our environments. That's not an easy task in this day and age.

As you look at the listed attributes and behaviors of the DiSC® tool, you might be better able to resonate with why our industry's uncertainty and ambiguity are so unsettling at times. Understanding not only our preset expectations for situations, but also our anticipated behaviors as people, often can provide personal insights, as well as a degree of relief, on why we feel uncomfortable with our profession's changing place in the industry.

Interestingly, we tend to have far less orientation toward steadiness and influence—perhaps surprising, given our caring, empathetic core beliefs and behaviors.

NOT JUST ANOTHER HEAD INJURY

Indeed, as the parents arrived at the bedside of their stricken son, it quickly became apparent to them both that normalcy for their family was gone forever. The caring, kind, and compassionate physicians and nurses were unable to penetrate the obvious grief of these parents easily. The more effort taken with communicating accurate descriptions of injuries, treatments, and prognoses, the higher their grief seemed to escalate, worsening the confusion.

Eventually, as the story unfolded, it became apparent the parents had significant health literacy problems despite a strong command of the English language. Both were naturalized citizens working hard to raise their family and to help advance the next generation. The outpouring of medical language, despite deep levels of caring, overwhelmed the capability of these parents to stay ahead of the situation, and their uncertainty led to an overwhelming feeling of ambiguity (and sense of guilt) for decisions needed with their son.

Decisions to terminate life support and proceed with organ donation are never made readily by any family. And they're certainly not ones to pursue with any degree of uncertainty or ambiguity.

As physicians, we must continually seek out the uncertainty in our patients' situations and be certain for ourselves that we have not been contributing—directly or indirectly—to any ambiguity that might have crept into their situations. Personal insight and increased awareness are essential steps for achieving improved leadership, not only for those we influence, but additionally for ourselves as humans.

I encourage all of us to continue seeking deeper levels of understanding for ourselves. As physician leaders, let us get more engaged, stay engaged, and help others to become engaged. Creating a broader level of positive change in healthcare—and society—is within our reach. Proactively helping others to better manage their transitions is a critical component of our professional responsibility, and in fact, it has been a professional responsibility since our beginnings.

REFERENCE

1. https://www.discprofile.com/what-is-disc/overview/

CHAPTER 16

Generation, Wisdom, and a Hero's Journey

Ongoing change in healthcare continues to create challenges for the physician workforce. Historically, many have viewed change through a lens of grievance while not considering how rising physicians might see opportunity. Society often sees physicians as heroes, and we must consider moving along a multistage path to find satisfaction with the outcomes of our hero's journey. Forgiveness, not simple acceptance, is essential.

A s we all know, there are usually four generations in the workforce at any point in time. In this era, sometimes, there actually can be five present. While we can recognize the differences among those generations, we often fail to integrate changes in our personal and professional behaviors to accommodate them. Each generation often complains about the inadequacies of the other generations—failing, more often than not, to acknowledge the accomplishments and special attributes of each. But the older can learn from the younger and, certainly, vice versa.

As physician leaders, we must not only apply knowledge of these differences to our patients as we decide how best to help them with their health issues, but also as we help our peers and others in the workforce adjust to these variations as well. Leadership most often is about influencing others to create improvements and adjustments that positively affect outcomes. Being aware of the recipients' expectations

ATTRIBUTES OF FIVE GENERATIONS

Traditionalists:

- Strengths and assets: strong work ethic, discipline, loyalty, emotional maturity
- Influences: Great Depression, World War II, G.I. Bill, Eisenhower, Korean War
- Information sources: Newspapers, books, peers, TV
- Learning styles: Traditional source of institutional knowledge
- Career planning: "I am happy to be where I am."

Baby Boomers:

- Strengths and assets: Customer service-focused, optimistic, dedicated, future-oriented
- Influences: Suburbia, Civil Rights Movement
- Information sources: TV, websites, newspapers
- Learning styles: Traditional learning, participation, reflection, feedback
- Career planning: "My dedication and service should be rewarded."

Generation X:

- Strengths and assets: Adaptability, tech literacy, creative, willing to buck the system
- Influences: – Challenger accident, gangs, internet, AIDS
- Information sources: – Websites, TV, books
- Learning styles: Highly receptive to e-learning, series of structured lectures
- Career planning: "It's about time I got a promotion."

Generation Y/Millennials:

- Strengths and assets: Optimistic, tech-savvy, global worldview, team player
- Influences: Oklahoma City bombing, rise of Facebook and Myspace, 9/11 attacks, high-speed internet
- Information sources: Email, social media
- Learning styles: Integrated technology and media
- Career planning: "If I give delivered results. I'll get promoted."

Generation Z:

- Strengths and assets: Digital native, service-oriented, receptive, culturally sensitive
- Influences: Social networking, mobile games, Columbine massacre, Boston Marathon bombing
- Information sources: Chat rooms, social media, YouTube
- Learning styles: Personalized learning through customized environments
- Career planning: "I'm smart, I'll get a job. I need a job."

or attitudes, and how best to adjust your approaches to those preset attitudes, can improve the outcomes of your leadership potential significantly.

Whether we recognize it or not, as physician leaders, we often are seen as heroes from many vantage points: our patients, our staff, our peers, our neighbors, our friends—and, yes, even our families. It is often too easy to become comfortable with the automatic and implied respect that comes with this role. Interestingly, the "physician hero" archetype crosses all generations; in the majority, each generation still views physicians in strongly optimistic ways. Our responsibilities therefore are significant.

What's a hero? By definition: a mythological or legendary figure, often of divine descent, endowed with great strength or ability; an illustrious warrior; a person admired for achievements and noble qualities; and/or one who shows great courage. And one could argue that physicians often are viewed by all levels of society in each of these ways at some level. Certainly, the public media can portray us this way.

James Bond seemed like a good hero when I was young and growing up. I read all of Ian Fleming's books in sequence and tried to emulate the behaviors I thought appropriate in trying to be a good Mr. Bond replicate. (And I will admit to having watched pretty much all of the movies available to this day.) Having grown up in Canada, I needed to deal with my divided loyalties of following too many hockey heroes as well: Jean Béliveau and Gordie Howe, to name only a couple. Homer's heroic tales, *The Iliad* and *The Odyssey*, were injected into my school readings as well. (I made attempts to read them again in later life but found them still somewhat boring, unfortunately.) And other heroes also have influenced me over time.

Being swayed by hero worship is natural for us all as we move through life.

TRANSFORMATIVE THRESHOLDS

Shifting gears slightly, with books such as *The Hero with a Thousand Faces*, *The Power of Myth*, and *The Inner Reaches of Outer Space*, Joseph Campbell reported on the synthesis he found while comparing the myths and legends of heroes in many cultures, writes Christopher Vogler in the foreword to *Myth & The Movies*, by Stuart Voytilla.[1] Vogler adds that the "hero's journey" was Campbell's all-embracing metaphor for the deep inner journey of transformation that heroes in every time and place seem to share, a path that leads them through great movements of separation, descent, ordeal, and return. While too lengthy to describe here, Campbell delineated 12 stages of the hero's journey, and these stages have been embraced by many as the most relevant paradigm for describing heroic journeys, including George Lucas in his Star Wars series.

This journey not only has stages of significance but also has thresholds a hero must cross to be transformed. A hero's response to the stages by his or her actions and decisions then creates the phases and pace of growth—a transformative leadership experience,

Why is this relevant to physician leadership?

Physicians, in our roles as leaders in healthcare, are on a hero's journey within the industry. For too long now, however, many physicians have used Elisabeth Kübler-Ross' five stages of grief as their paradigm for the ongoing changes in healthcare:

1. **Denial:** The first stage wherein the individual believes the diagnosis is mistaken and clings to a false, preferable reality.

2. **Anger:** The individual recognizes denial cannot continue and instead becomes frustrated, especially at proximate individuals. Possible responses: "Why me? It's not fair!" and "Who is to blame?"

3. **Bargaining:** The individual hopes to avoid a cause of grief. Often, the negotiation for an extended life is made in exchange for a reformed lifestyle. People facing less-serious trauma frequently seek compromise.

4. **Depression:** The individual despairs at recognition of his or her mortality. In this state, the individual may become silent, refuse visitors, and spend much of his or her time mournful and sullen.

5. **Acceptance:** In the final stage, the individual embraces his or her mortality or inevitable future, or that of a loved one, or another tragic event. People dying may precede the survivors in this state.

And that is where the understanding of what is happening has frequently stopped—simply trying to accept the complexity and ongoing change in our industry.

I would suggest this is an older, generational approach and that we all—every generation in the workforce—now need to consider how better to move along in our hero journey. By accepting there is more than simple "acceptance" of the inevitable, we can individually (and collectively) help advance our discipline more successfully and collaboratively, and with additional positive expectations of the outcomes from our hero journey.

Each generation can help the others cross a threshold to a new stage of improved healthcare delivery—and an improved approach in our philosophies for how to deliver better care with compassion, empathy, and kindness to our patients, our peers, and our fellow workers within this industry we influence so deeply. Let's learn how to listen more closely to one another; there is much to learn.

LETTING THE PAST GO

I readily accept that physician workforce morale is at an all-time low. However, simply accepting will not be enough if we, as heroes, are going to create the change the industry expects of its natural leaders. With morale such as it is, forgiveness also becomes a component of transformation we need to consider.

A delightful, short read in fable format is a book by physician Robert C. Stone. *Circle of Wisdom: A Path for Life, Mind and Leadership.*[2]

It characterizes how we can gain wisdom continually as we accept the need for inevitable change and routinely prepare ourselves for constant change, not only in our lives but with our circumstances as they present themselves. I've attempted to characterize the circle of wisdom from a fable here:

> Awareness for change needed → Willingness for change to occur → Creation of actual change → Forgiveness after change outcomes

The first three parts are intuitively obvious. Moving to the fourth step and then back to the first one for the next cycle of change is less intuitive. It is more complicated because it embraces the concept of forgiveness—another topic we can't fully cover here. The essence, however, is that to move forward with change, we must cross a threshold in which the past is let go. Similar to the hero's journey, this crossing is essential for forward progress. In this case, the act of forgiveness is not only about forgiving the external influences that affect you, but also forgiving oneself for all past actions, attitudes, and behaviors. By forgiving ourselves, we can move to a new phase of personal growth and become prepared for the next set of influences that inevitably cross our paths.

We all should be proud of what physician leadership represents in healthcare. We all have the opportunity to continue building our own skills to become more fluid with the ever-changing environments as we all strive for improvements to the industry. We cannot expect positive personal change if we continue to hold onto elements of the past and keep trying to re-create a time that already has moved beyond our expectations.

By considering the combination of generational differences and how to collaborate across generations better, coupled with understanding and proactively pursuing a hero's journey and then also injecting a heavy dose of forgiveness, our path toward increased wisdom can be influenced positively. A net potential result is that physicians can achieve larger scales of change for themselves, our peers, and for the industry as a whole—with patients benefiting from improved quality, safety, and efficiency in more-compassionate environments.

REFERENCES

1. Voytilla S. *Myths & the Movies*. Michael Wiese Productions; 1999.
2. Stone RC. *Circle of Wisdom: A Path for Life, Mind and Leadership*. CreateSpace Independent Publishing Platform; 2015.

CHAPTER 17

Crisis Management and Catastrophes: Times for Learning?

Natural catastrophes and societal crises seem to have occupied much attention. No doubt, there have been many lives and communities affected on both small- and large scales. What do these events offer physician leaders? The onus remains on physicians to guide our industry forward—an industry some say is in crisis mode.

In December 2019, an online search showed about 216 million results were found on Google in 0.51 seconds for "crisis management plan," about 15.8 million results were found in 0.53 seconds for "catastrophe management plan," and about 206 million results in 0.81 seconds for "disaster management plan." Clearly, any attempt to academically review greater than a half-billion results to learn something more would be catastrophic in itself. I needed another path.

Most of us have been aware of disaster planning efforts for our medical facilities and within our office environments. We might even have something organized for our homes and families. And yet most of us also are aware of how imperfect those plans are and how poorly they might reflect the reality of any particular situation. Rehearsal and practicing help modulate those potential nuances, but every situation is different. For instance, just consider how we all react whenever the darned fire alarm happens in our workplaces.

I am not going to take on the debate as to whether healthcare is in crisis mode—everyone is entitled to their opinions and viewpoints. I will state, however, that healthcare is an inherently complex industry and so it is easy for both optimistic and pessimistic viewpoints to emerge. Optimism tends to bring views for opportunity, while pessimism can bring views toward protectionism (also debatable). This complexity is an opportunity for physician leadership and our profession to emerge continuously as a significantly important influence for the industry to follow. The industry precedent is in place, and expectations for physicians to lead remains strong at multiple levels in our societies. In fact, physician leadership is now a strong market demand in many environments and communities as it relates to healthcare delivery.

LEARNING HAPPENS EVERYWHERE

As a business school guest lecturer. I was privileged to present the topic of physician leadership to a crowd of more than 200 graduate students and faculty from nonclinical disciplines related to healthcare (MHA, MPH, etc.). Looking out from the lectern, it was obvious even before I got into the message of my presentation that I was being held in high regard just because the audience knew I was a physician who had embraced leadership as a career path—humbling, for sure. The lecture went fine, the questions were poignant, and the swarm after the talk was gratifying. But my ego aside, the real learning moment for me—not the audience members—was in watching their enthusiasm to engage in our industry and their energy for wanting to help create further change in this complex set of systems. I left the event feeling optimistic about their futures, and ours as physicians, that we have a fresh generation coming into the field, and that their impact soon will be felt.

We already know that those entering medical school and residency programs continue to carry high levels of altruism and idealism.

They, too, are driven to create change and, as best possible, to make improvements beyond simple patient care. So if there is any form of crisis pending out there, it might be one where we, who are already in the workforce, are not effectively laying the groundwork for younger generations to more easily and readily succeed as they make their presence felt in the workforce. It is a necessity that we learn how to avert this form of a crisis so that our industry, our future peers and our patients all can benefit from the effects of these individuals as well.

Let's pay attention; the younger generation has much to teach, and we all have much to learn from up-and-coming clinicians and other affiliated healthcare disciplines. Interprofessional approaches will only grow.

AN INDUSTRY CRISIS

A crisis in workforce wellness also is present in our industry, and it is present within all disciplines—clinical and nonclinical. Our workforces are getting worn out with this industry's complexity and the difficulties with creating change in its systems. One easily can list all the changes needed and areas where innovation is required, but this will continue to take some time. For example, the current era of patient safety and quality is nearing 20 years. Have we made significant change in these areas? That, too, is debatable, but our workforces are getting tired in their efforts to keep making necessary changes. Large-scale industry change typically takes three to four generations of time. So what can we collectively learn?

I would advocate more simplicity, not more complexity, in the varying approaches to systems reengineering. There already is a robust science out there we need to embrace. We also need to further embrace the science for human-factors engineering to create significant change and to also incorporate the evolving science of behavioral decision-making in our efforts. These are only a couple of example areas, and I recognize it is far too easy to state their need versus actually implementing projects in this regard. Nonetheless, there is much to learn from these disciplines that we should consider integrating within healthcare.

Financial reform and realignment is another area where we can create learning opportunity. Finances drive the entire system, by necessity. Fortunately, payers in both the for-profit and public sectors are making efforts toward value-based care and payment. Once more, however, I would advocate for increased simplicity with the large number of financial models being trialed by various organizations. Let's learn to walk before we run with value-based care strategies and financial reform. That does not mean go slowly; it just means we should try to make success occur with simpler solutions that can be replicated before we advocate for the widespread, multiple pathways or experimental models. (Payers are guilty of these approaches.) Shotgun strategies only serve to confuse the marketplace and also create the risk for profiteering.

I encourage all of us to continue seeking deeper levels of optimism and to generate positive influence at all levels to which we are individually comfortable

And as we continue to make change in healthcare, let us not forget about the many individuals and communities who have been, and who will in the future be, affected by crises or catastrophes. At their core, all physicians are caring, compassionate people who care deeply about others. Let your own altruism and idealism surface so that others are aware all around you, so that you can help others in their moments of need during difficult times. It is what we do—it is our calling to help and care for others that benefits society.

CHAPTER 18

Physicians Meeting the Challenge of Contrasting Ideologies

Clinical care delivery often is challenging and, at times, requires numerous opinions. Implicit bias can enter into the process and make optimal decisions difficult to recognize. With discussion, however, consensus can be reached. The same holds true for management and leadership. In both contexts, there are multiple situations and scenarios every day that require consensus.

Our nation's healthcare industry is more complex than all other industries and will continue to be complex and create significant uncertainty. Such complexity, interestingly, seems to occur regardless of political leanings or opinions, but this uncertainty means that large numbers of patients and their families are being negatively affected.

Remember: The number one reason why people file for bankruptcy continues to be related to healthcare debt.[1]

Growing up in Midwest North America, I distinctly remember a multitude of societal opinions that often carried distinct bias and deeply engrained ideology. Of course, while I was young, I did not understand these words, let alone the nature of the behaviors they represented. Going through medical school, I gradually became aware of these human attributes and how they impacted not only clinical care but also management decisions that eventually influenced educational approaches. For example, our medical school class was subjected to a unilateral decision that we all had to receive BCG vaccination against tuberculosis. At the time, it was a relatively untested approach of unproven value—and no member of the class was given the option of not receiving the vaccination. Given the nature of our training environment at the time, and the social diversity of patients passing through the system, I still argue that this was not a public health-oriented decision, but one of implicit bias and regional ideology within the leadership of the school.

Behaviors, or actions, are predicated on individual and collective values, beliefs, and ideals. Behaviors influence our cultures and ultimately the environments within which we live, work, and play. Leadership, and the behavior of leaders, is what influences a culture most significantly. Creating a healthy culture is pivotal for improving the healthcare industry, and healthcare leadership must take special care to manage implicit biases and contrasting ideologies through exceptional behavior.

VALUES, BELIEFS, IDEALS, AND MORE

Perhaps it's a bit remedial, but covering a few basic definitions can be a helpful reminder about what drives our behaviors and actions.

- **Values:** Important and lasting beliefs or ideals shared by the members of a culture about what is good or bad and desirable or undesirable. (Source: *Business Dictionary*)
- **Beliefs:** Assumptions and convictions that are held to be true by an individual or a group, regarding concepts, events, people and things. (Source: *Business Dictionary*)
- **Ideals:** Persons or things conceived as embodying such a conception, and conforming to such a standard, they are taken as a model for imitation. (Source: Dictionary.com)

- **Ideology:** A system of ideas that explains and lends legitimacy to actions and beliefs of a social, religious, political, or corporate entity. (Source: *Business Dictionary*)
- **Implicit bias:** Refers to the attitudes or stereotypes that affect our understanding, actions, and decisions in an unconscious manner. These biases, which encompass both favorable and unfavorable assessments, are activated involuntarily and without an individual's awareness or intentional control. (Source: Kirwan Institute for the Study of Race and Ethnicity, Ohio State University.)
- **Consensus:** The middle ground in decision-making, between total assent and total disagreement. It depends upon participants having shared values and goals, and on having broad agreement on specific issues and overall direction. It implies everyone accepts and supports the decision, and understands the reasons for making it. (Source: *Business Dictionary*)

LEADERSHIP IS ALWAYS ABOUT PEOPLE

Patient care is all about people. Clinical delivery systems are all about teams of people working well together. And the patient-physician relationship remains one of the most intimate, trusted, and caring of human relationships known.

All physicians are leaders at some level, and leadership is ultimately about people—regardless of clinical discipline or nonclinical activity. The leadership that physicians provide, whether informally or formally, is still a dominant influence for the culture of healthcare.

The values, beliefs, and ideals of physician behavior remain central to one of our profession's sacred guides, the Hippocratic Oath; it is perhaps the most widely known of Greek medical texts. The oath requires physicians to promise to uphold a number of professional ethical standards. Here are a few excerpts:

"In purity and according to divine law will I carry out my life and my art."

"Into whatever homes I go, I will enter them for the benefit of the sick, avoiding any voluntary act of impropriety or corruption, including the seduction of women or men, whether they are free men or slaves."

"Whatever I see or hear in the lives of my patients, whether in connection with my professional practice or not, which ought not to be spoken of outside, I will keep secret, as considering all such things to be private."

"So long as I maintain this oath faithfully and without corruption, may it be granted to me to partake of life fully and the practice of my art, gaining the respect of all men for all time."

Let us all reinvigorate in consideration of that oath as we seek ways to augment the professionalism that has carried the health and culture of the industry for so many generations. Incoming physicians, and those established in careers, readily gravitate to the altruistic side of the spectrum for these values, beliefs, and ideals. It is our collective altruism that shapes our individual as well as collective behaviors. Altruism can be considered a core ideology for physicians.

The past few decades have challenged physicians' roles in healthcare and in society as a whole. The recent shift to a value-based model of care delivery is likely to survive and become the predominant focus for care delivery. Compared to the recent past, physicians now have a fresh opportunity to demonstrate leadership at all levels. The opportunity for influence by physicians will help shape the evolving culture of healthcare in coming years. Physicians value "value."

ADAPTING FOR PERPETUAL CHANGE

The inherent complexity of healthcare creates the perpetual expectation for change. We must all be comfortable with this reality. Even with the variety of value-based approaches on our horizon, significant swings in our industry already are occurring. As another important figure from ancient Greek history, the philosopher Heraclitus, once said, "The only constant is change." That readily applies to healthcare.

The vagaries of national politics contribute to constant change, regardless of which party is in control. Obviously, physicians will have opinions and debates not only on politics in general, but also on the impact of politics on healthcare specifically. In these discussions, contrasting ideologies certainly will surface and, at times, create consternation.

As leaders, physicians also have the opportunity to use their influence to facilitate healthy, balanced discussions while also helping their local, regional, or national environments achieve stability in the face of contrasting ideologies. Again, physicians are leaders, and leaders create culture through their influence—not only in their decisions but also through their individual, daily behaviors. Physician-oriented values, beliefs, and ideals can provide the voice of reason when contrasting ideologies are present. Where change is constant, leadership also should be constant—to provide the optimal pathway through shifting circumstances. Physicians are positioned to provide balance and direction within healthcare during periods of intense change. Let us all rise to the occasion and not become excessively distracted by contrasting ideologies. (To quote another popular phrase: "May the Force be with you.")

While pursuing my academic career in trauma surgery, followed now by more than a decade of leadership roles nationally and internationally, I have come to realize that contrasting ideologies are always active on a routine basis. The implicit biases that are related to them create the diversity of opinion that ultimately makes our world so special. Navigating ideology and implicit bias are a portion of my daily routine. In so doing, I must always be introspective and on an internal lookout for how my own implicit bias may (or may not) create decisions that are not fully optimal.

To help offset my propensity of implicit bias and ideology, I routinely seek a variety of opinions from a variety of sources that I know will not be similar to mine. I believe this is what successful leaders should do in order to make their best decisions, regardless of leadership style. Building consensus becomes simpler and decision-making more robust.

Coming from a background in surgery, it has been an interesting process to continually unlearn my inherently developed surgical personality traits . . . and it is an ongoing process, believe me!

Helping to proactively manage transitions in our industry is a critical component of our professional responsibility; in fact, it has been a professional responsibility since our beginnings.

REFERENCE

1. https://ajph.aphapublications.org/doi/abs/10.2105/AJPH.2018.304901?journal Code=ajph

CHAPTER 19

Patient-Centered Care: Is It Really Disruption?

Patient-centered care is a common industry term that resonates deeply, yet truly successful implementation of it remains an enigma for most patient-care environments. Physician-centered care is the ongoing standard for how delivery systems are organized, and this organizational dependency on physician centricity creates a paradox between consistency of known delivery models and adaptation of new models of care. Managing this paradox is disruptive and will be an industry challenge for some time yet.

HISTORIC PRECEDENT

Being somewhat of an idealist and altruistic individual, as a surgical trainee in Montreal at McGill University, I was highly influenced by a seemingly omnipresent influence of William Osler. The Osler Library is located at McGill University's Medical School, and the auditorium where our surgical educational sessions were conducted had a large portrait of Osler hanging in constant view. Like many, I endeavored to emulate his teachings and to practice by those ideologies. I just couldn't shake his stare from that portrait—you know, the type of portrait where the eyes are always following you.

Sir William Osler (1849-1919) was a Canadian physician who created the first residency program for specialty training of physicians, and he brought medical students out of the lecture hall for bedside clinical training. He frequently has been described as the "Father of Modern Medicine," and his career traversed the universities of McGill (1874-1884), Pennsylvania (1884-1889), Johns Hopkins (1889-1905), and Oxford (1905-1919).

A prolific writer, he once wrote in an essay titled *Books and Men* that, "He who studies medicine without books sails an uncharted sea, but he who studies medicine without patients does not go to sea at all." He also is credited for saying, "Listen to your patient; he is telling you the diagnosis," emphasizing the need to take a good history.

In a similar vein of thought, who in medicine hasn't heard of Florence Nightingale? Her influence on patient care has been omnipresent in our industry, primarily through her role in founding the modern nursing profession. Nightingale (1820-1910) rose to prominence managing nurses she trained during the Crimean War, where she organized the tending of wounded soldiers and gave nursing a highly favorable reputation. She became the iconic "Lady with the Lamp" while making rounds at night.

An English social reformer and statistician, Nightingale established a nursing school at London's St. Thomas' Hospital in 1860. Now part of King's College London, it was the world's first secular nursing school. Also a prolific writer, she worked to improve healthcare for all sections of British society, advocate hunger relief in India, abolish prostitution laws that were overly harsh to women, and expand female employment. In partial recognition of her pioneering work, new nurses take the Nightingale Pledge. She helped set an example of compassion and commitment to patient care, as well as diligent and thoughtful hospital administration. Indeed, patient-centered care actually has been a focus for roughly 150 years.

A DISRUPTIVE FUTURE

Patient-centered care is taking on new meaning, however, while the primary focus on physicians being the dominant conduit for care and decision-making remains. Since the mid-to-late 1800s, the complexities of healthcare delivery systems have escalated logarithmically. We all know, and feel, the diversity of influences (too many to list) that now encroach the core components of essential patient care—the patient-physician relationship and the patient-nurse relationship in a conducive environment for optimal care.

A portion of what is gradually occurring is the rapid adoption of technologies and the progressive implementation of not only expanded responsibilities for non-physician providers but also an expanded number of non-physician clinicians involved with patient care. Several components of a new paradox gradually are becoming clearer—the paradox between existing delivery systems oriented toward how altruistic physicians prefer to deliver care versus a renewed focus on patient-centered care that is trying to thrive in a highly complex set of evolving systems amid new types of providers not yet fully oriented to patients.

Disruption of our industry is at the core of this paradox. Learning to manage it effectively will be a challenge for physician leadership and everyone oriented toward truly successful patient-centered care.

ARE WE COMMUNICATING PROPERLY?

Communication, communication, communication . . . we all know it's an essential component of healthcare. When things go incredibly well, communication, caring, and compassion are most often at the core of success. Equally, however, when things go horribly wrong in healthcare, communication problems are usually at the core.

Among many examples, electronic health records gradually have gained acceptance in healthcare. Cloud-based data warehousing and assertive efforts with data analytics are common practices. Push messaging that results from the analytics is now prevalent. Social media channels are generally accepted, and expected, forms of communication. But what is less clear is the collective and eventual impact on healthcare delivery, especially when patient expectations are higher than provider willingness.

Our personal lives have been pervasively affected—and relatively quickly—by technology as all generations are now seemingly dependent on digital devices for information, and a new form of addictive dependency apparently is evolving. Interpersonal communication and the types of relationships being formed are in unprecedented transition. A new type of patient-physician relationship is developing gradually, but is not yet formalized.

TECHNOLOGY TROUBLES

The Internet is propelling clinicians into new ethical and legal territory, raising questions about the accuracy of online information, patients' right to privacy, and doctors' liability regarding their patients' online behavior.

Liliya Gershengoren, a psychiatrist and professor with Weill Cornell Medicine, concluded from a survey she conducted that an overwhelming majority of psychiatrists and residents at one U.S. academic hospital had Googled a patient at some point in their careers. These survey results were presented at the American Psychiatric Association's 2016 annual meeting.[1]

Of 48 staff doctors and 34 residents who responded anonymously, 93% of staff and 94% of residents reported researching a patient online at least once. She found that 17% of staff and 40% of residents Googled their patients on a frequent or semiregular basis in the emergency department (compared to 5% of staff and 15% of residents in inpatient settings).

And then there are external risks—malevolent forces that continually try to create chaos by penetrating our organizational technology with the intention of stealing patient data, holding patient care networks for ransom, or even doing harm to patients.

As physicians, we must continually seek how to optimize patient-centered care in the face of ever-increasing change and complexity. We must also continue to seek how our role as the natural, intended leaders in the healthcare system (and the dominant focus of patient care) can be further optimized. Increased personal awareness in both these areas will be essential for achieving improved outcomes on both fronts. Managing any paradox is not about "yes" or "no" decisions—it is a process of finding, then managing, the balance for both the individuals and organizations we influence within it. Positive outcomes often result from disruption.

I encourage all of us to continue seeking deeper levels of understanding. As physician leaders, let us get more engaged, stay engaged, and help others to become engaged. Creating a broader level of positive change in healthcare and society is within our reach. Proactively helping others, as physician leaders, to better manage the disruptive paradox of true patient-centered care is a critical component of our professional responsibility—in fact, it has been a professional responsibility since our beginnings.

REFERENCE

1. https://www.psychcongress.com/article/most-psychiatric-professionals-google-their-patients-survey-finds

CHAPTER 20

Physicians and the Sense of Accomplishment

Practicing medicine is a science and an art! Physicians ascribe to this routinely, and throughout our careers seek ways in which to gain professional and personal satisfaction in both. Healthcare as an industry is challenging but also highly rewarding. And yet at times it can impede the ability of physicians to achieve their hoped for degrees of satisfaction. As leaders, reframing context and challenges in a positive direction of growth may help provide better outcomes—for our patients, staff, friends, and, importantly, for ourselves and our families.

At our most simple human core, we all want to feel safe, be healthy, stay happy, and be able to live our lives with ease and minimal discomfort. Sure, we all have other wants, but at our core, these four areas are pivotal. Some days we can forget just how privileged we are and become preoccupied by how our higher desires are not met. Taking a moment to appreciate these simple core areas for ourselves and then purposefully choosing to be happy in our lives helps to minimize the times when we feel our other wants are not being met.

HAPPINESS OFTEN CAN BE JUST A SIMPLE CHOICE

For myself, while I remain fully committed to professional growth, I also recognize that expanding my personal growth clearly provides extra tangible benefits toward my professional life. As a younger man, I spent countless hours in the outdoors. As happens, higher education, family, and career created alternate paths that provided levels of higher satisfaction, and my proximity to the outdoors faded somewhat.

But when I reached that proverbial mid-career stage in my 50s, I also realized that reaching back to some of my core areas as an individual could refresh my view for personal satisfaction, improved positivity, and spiritual growth. This came about in the form of pursuing the outdoors again and finding ways to explore activities I missed when younger—mountaineering is one.

While summiting a few peaks in the gorgeous Canadian Rockies, I found myself reflecting on why the experience was so joyful. Turns out it is not just the scenery. In fact, there also can be potential parallels to our pursuit of medicine as a career path.

By nature, we are high achievers. At our professional core, we all want to succeed in the science and art of medicine. We also want to continue moving closer toward matured approaches of true patient-centered care. These professional pursuits generally are high in satisfaction. But there also is ongoing data emerging on the negative morale issues in the physician workforce that may often start as early as medical school.

At times, our evolving industry does not make it any easier to remain optimistic, positive, and highly energized. Keeping the joy and meaning in our work can be difficult. As physician leaders, helping ourselves and others to reframe the context of these challenges can be helpful.

It so happens that individuals who pursue mountaineering often have similar personality traits as physicians in terms of their personal ego drive and need for a sense of accomplishment. An article written in the *Canadian Alpine Journal* entitled "The 7Cs of Mountaineering Experience[1] captures some of these attributes from which I will attempt (perhaps poorly) to draw those parallels:

1. **Challenge:** Being a physician has significant intellectual, physical, and psychological demands. These demands are present from pre-medical training and persist throughout our careers in a variety of ways. How we manage these demands often contributes to our sense of accomplishment. Equally, how we are unable to effectively manage them can contribute to a sense of frustration, and it is important to delineate what challenges we are directly able to influence versus those we cannot. If we cannot, then our appreciation that we are not failing as individuals is critical to recognize. Challenges are actually opportunities for potential success that are thinly disguised. Leaders are able to recognize these as real opportunities for success.

2. **Control:** This is often related to how we perceive the ability to successfully manage our own destiny and, for physicians, carries a strong desire to be self-reliant. Most of us were trained to be independent, autonomous decision-makers, and we measure our success in this regard. Gradually this is changing, however, with various generational preferences for learning and interacting in groups. Multi-professional teams also are emerging, and there are pressures to have patient care decided by non-physicians at times. Overall, we must continue to adjust and effectively adapt in these changing environments where we don't hold complete control. Being able to influence processes and outcomes can be accomplished without full control and is a specially developed leadership skill in itself.

3. **Community:** Regardless of our interests, a natural human instinct is to participate with a community. Data shows that individuals engaged with communities tend to live longer and appreciate more satisfying lives. Being a physician has often been referred to as a "brotherhood/sisterhood" of sorts. As the most highly educated medical professionals, it is natural to feel this kinship, and our society reinforces this with its view of high regard for the profession.

It is an honor and privilege to hold this spot in society, but it also is one that our profession should continue to humbly cherish as a privilege not to be lost by ineffective leadership.

4. **Context:** Generally, this refers to settings where any type of activity takes place or the influence present on that setting or activity. For physicians, this can be the most complex to grasp and to remain comfortable with because the context of the industry is multi-factorial and ever-changing. Recognizing this as context in itself can be helpful for many physicians; there is no stable environment for healthcare. This does not mean physicians should be fatalistic and just accept the current context. It should be quite the opposite, actually. We are in a period of healthcare where the voice of physician leadership (at all levels) is needed and, more importantly, wanted and being actively sought by delivery systems, payers, policymakers, governmental bodies. and vendors. It is a unique opportunity for physician leadership and ready to be embraced in its full context.

5. **Creative Opportunity:** This is where the ability to make decisions and think creatively with confidence exists. Physicians have this opportunity on a routine basis, and it is often referenced in the catchphrase "medicine is an art and a science." The ongoing development of guidelines and measurement strategies will not disappear; but I believe there still remains opportunity through physician leadership to positively impact and influence the science of guidelines and measurement that accommodates the "art-form" of clinical decision-making. As a workforce, we need to engage further in this regard. Parenthetically, many physicians also demonstrate high levels of artistic output separate from being in medicine, or they pursue the enjoyment of numerous activities to better connect with this creativity drive present within.

6. **Catharsis:** This can be related to an eventual internal sense of relief and relaxation that provides a feeling of freedom and simplification.

As physician leaders in today's environment, this can be difficult to recognize and may be lost in the busyness of clinical care and administrative duties. Stepping back professionally to recognize positive clinical outcomes with difficult cases can be highly rejuvenating and should be sought as best possible. Internally satisfying avocations can help one connect with this sense of inner calm and will also help remind oneself how to recognize this same sense of peace when professionally active. Formal mindfulness practices are also important potential adjuncts in this regard for many. Personal leadership is critical.

7. **Chrysalis:** This is a bit of metaphorical stretch referencing the shell that a caterpillar emerges from as a new butterfly and represents metamorphosis with redevelopment. To some degree this can also be recognized as being related to the outcomes of catharsis. For physicians, providing patient care and participating with successful systems of care delivery often creates the development of an ongoing spiritual and therapeutic connection that routinely provides life-affirming changes. We do what we do because of the immense positive change we are able to create for others. There is ever-present change in healthcare and the industry forever will be inherently complex. Recognizing that change is constant actually provides each of us with the opportunity to embrace and anticipate a regular series of metamorphoses in a career path. This recognition in itself can be enlightening. Leadership, too, often is about facilitating the metamorphosis of others during these periods of persistent and ongoing change—personally and professionally.

Regardless of your career stage or chronological age, it is important to routinely reflect on your core values, ideals and beliefs. There is also opportunity to reframe the context of your environment and your challenges in a positive direction. This reframing may also help provide better outcomes—for our patients, staff, friends, and, most importantly, ourselves and our families.

Helping to manage proactively transitions in our industry is a critical component of our professional responsibility. In fact, it has been a professional responsibility since our beginning.

REFERENCE

1. Benjamin M, Quinn M. The 7Cs of mountaineering experience. *Canadian Alpine Journal.* 2016;99

CHAPTER 21

Telehealth: Has Its Time Arrived?

Telemedicine has been around for decades, but new uses for it are emerging rapidly.

While a medical student during the late 1970s in Midwestern Canada, videoconferencing to remote practices was routine during grand rounds, with the occasional added presentation of patients. As a student, I assumed that was standard practice. I soon learned that was certainly not the case.

I never saw those practices again until many years later as a faculty member at Yale University in the mid-1990s, where I participated with NASA-funded research as a portion of NASA's ongoing efforts with telemedicine. A mandate that has guided NASA since the early 1960s has been the space agency's push for commercialization of telemedicine technology in order to spin off the benefits of human space flight and other scientific or technical endeavors.[1]

To better facilitate this mandate, the agency sponsored the creation of a Commercial Space Center named the Medical Informatics and Technology Applications Consortium (MITAC) at Yale University in the mid-1990s. At the MITAC, we not only pursued a range of telehealth projects but, most important, created a variety of different terrestrial test beds for new technology in the remote locations of Ecuador, Russia, and the Arctic.[2]

For those with a historical bent, the roots of telemedicine are entwined with the agency's earliest days and the modern history of human space flight. The dominant medical question prior to Yuri Gagarin's successful space flight in April 1961 was whether the human body could function in space. In particular, physicians were concerned that the removal of gravity would impede circulation and respiration. (For more on space medicine during the Mercury, Gemini, and Apollo programs see Mae Mills Link, *Space Medicine in Project Mercury*, Washington, DC: National Aeronautics and Space Administration Special Publication-4003, 1965; and John Pitts, *The Human Factor: Biomedicine in the Manned Space Program to 1980*, Washington, DC: National Aeronautics and Space Administration Special Publication Special Publication-4213, 1985.)

Formally defined by the American Telemedicine Association, telemedicine is synonymous with telehealth and is the use of medical information exchanged from one site to another via electronic communications to improve a patient's clinical health status. Telemedicine is not a separate medical specialty.

Products and services related to telemedicine often are part of a larger investment by healthcare institutions in information technology or the delivery of clinical care.

CHANGE PROMPTS INNOVATION

Why does this industry have such continuous change? There's no easy answer to that question. However, one significant component is that, at its core in America, healthcare remains a free-market economy. Moreover, in this economy on the clinical delivery side there is at least a 30% waste and inefficiency rate. There also remains significantly high levels of error in patient care despite 15 years of concerted efforts to address patient safety in U.S. healthcare.

It is estimated that 15 to 20 sectors exist within the healthcare industry beyond the clinical delivery components. Given the rates of error and inefficiencies, these sectors are often seeking to capitalize on a business opportunity—some altruistically and others not so much.

It is now abundantly clear on the clinical delivery side that the ongoing transition from a volume-based payment system to one focused on value has gained momentum and will not be reversed. Equally, government and for-profit payers are rolling out new value-based payment programs and products with intense speed and aggressive timelines.

Collectively, this creates the potential for confusion while the system is challenged and tries to adapt to a rapidly changing environment. Traditional paradigms and practices are quickly disappearing. Opportunists will continue to blossom. Innovation is essential.

Telemedicine is one innovation that appears to be taking off. (For a timely podcast link, Is Telehealth the New Black?, visit https://www.soundpracticepodcast.com/e/is-telehealth-the-new-black/.)

The need for novel approaches to healthcare delivery is essential. Physicians will clearly help drive the changes and transitions to new approaches. Physician leadership is critical to make sure the opportunities are capitalized upon.

Leaders usually seek innovative solutions to ongoing flux or change within systems and industries. Telehealth is not so much a new innovation at this time, but the opportunity to leverage its innovative potential is certainly present more than previously.

But telehealth also represents something bigger. It is the opportunity to conceptualize healthcare differently. By thinking differently, other novel approaches to healthcare delivery will also surface. The roles of clinicians in these new delivery models will also change. Physicians thinking differently can be the nidus for important changes. Be the change agents!

REFERENCES

1. NASA Spinoff. http://spinoff.nasa.gov/spinhist.html.
2. The Medical Informatics and Technology Applications Consortium. http://www.meditac.com.

CHAPTER 22

Trust: Professionalism, Altruism, Forbearance

In times of uncertainty, human behavior often makes people resort to less-than-stellar behaviors; unhealthy personal environments can become manifest as well. Often, these coincide with healthcare being used more frequently and the safe haven of healthcare delivery being sought. With all physicians being leaders, it is incumbent upon us to demonstrate a variety of professional qualities, and we must also draw on our own human qualities to succeed as well.

"Philosophy does not promise to secure anything external for man, otherwise it would be admitting something that lies beyond its proper subject matter. For as the material of the carpenter is wood, and that of statuary bronze, so the subject matter of the art of living is each person's own life."

— EPICTETUS
Discourses 1.15.2

It was during a particularly difficult end-of-life family discussion a few years back that I was reacquainted with just how hostile patient families can behave in the hospital environment at times. The exact details are not important now, but the near-frenzied altercation resulted in my having to alert our more-senior hospital leadership of the situation. While heading toward the C-suite, a kindly pastor who had witnessed the events sidled up beside me for the walk down "mahogany row."

The pastor had assumed I needed consoling and was there to offer spiritual support, or so she thought. What took the pastor by surprise was my comment somewhat along the lines of, "I am always impressed by how the people who are creating the most grief for me at any point are the same people who help me to learn the most about my thoughts and attitudes." To my surprise, the pastor seemed shocked by this approach and was curious about why this was my philosophy toward difficult situations. Apparently, this particular pastor had not yet been exposed to alternatives of thought when faced with complex situations or difficult families. Consolation was a more operative approach for her.

Subsequently, once the situation settled with all parties calmed and the institution being looked upon favorably by the family, the pastor and I settled into a discourse on professionalism as the combination of all the qualities that are connected with trained and skilled people. In so doing, we both came to appreciate how different our individual philosophies were and how they had been so strongly shaped by the professional expectations set during our respective training. It also encouraged me to always respect how, as physicians, we each need to listen for the differences out there and to see what can be learned from others—professional or nonprofessional.

The words "profession" and "professional" come from the Latin word *professio*, which means a public declaration with the force of a promise. The traditional professions are medicine, law, education, and clergy. The marks of a profession are:[1]

- Competence in a specialized body of knowledge and skill;
- An acknowledgment of specific duties and responsibilities toward the individuals it serves and toward society; and
- The right to train, admit, discipline, and dismiss its members for failure to sustain competence or observe the duties and responsibilities.

Professionalism requires that practitioners strive for excellence in the following areas, which should be modeled by mentors and teachers and become part of the attitudes, behaviors and skills integral to patient care:[1]

- **Altruism:** A physician is obligated to attend to the best interest of patients, rather than self-interest.
- **Accountability:** Physicians are accountable to their patients, to society on issues of public health, and to their profession.
- **Excellence:** Physicians are obligated to make a commitment to lifelong learning.
- **Duty:** A physician should be available and responsive when "on call," accepting a commitment to service within the profession and the community.
- **Honor and integrity:** Physicians should be committed to being fair, truthful and straightforward in their interactions with patients and the profession.
- **Respect for others:** A physician should demonstrate respect for patients and their families, other physicians and team members, medical students, residents and fellows.

Of these six areas, each strikes a chord that resonates deeply. But for me, it is altruism that continues to provide the most resonance for continuing on the professional route chosen. By definition, altruism is the attitude of caring about others and doing acts that help them, although one does not get anything for himself or herself by doing those acts. For whatever reason in my core psychology, altruism seems to help me in times of duress and certainly provides a sense of personal comfort even during times of success. I trust and depend on my altruism as a consistent compass bearing—a proverbial true north, if you will.

However, as we all recognize, in today's healthcare industry, there is clearly much to be concerned about and so many complexities to manage among a wide range of competing priorities. Idealism is easy to speak of, and yet quite difficult to enact upon on a regular basis. Our patience and commitment to the six components of professionalism are challenged on a daily basis routinely. And many of our peers are struggling with maintaining balanced views on professional and personal issues. We are indeed in a period of time when challenges may often seem to be more common than successes.

With this complexity, there is an even greater need for each of us (young or old) to look deep into what drives us as physicians. What drives us to be leaders in society? What makes us want to create larger change in the world? And what kinds of changes—or resurrection of core beliefs—are needed by each of us to make our chosen profession more satisfying? It's a profession that still carries the opportunity for us to achieve that intense professional satisfaction we all know exists.

From time to time, I will read about the ancient Stoic philosophies. Stoicism teaches the development of self-control and fortitude as a means of overcoming destructive emotions. The philosophy holds that becoming a clear and unbiased thinker allows one to understand the universal reason (logos).

One such concept within Stoicism is that of "forbearance," a term describing the quality of being patient and being able to forgive someone or to control oneself in a difficult situation. I bring this up in the context of professionalism and altruism because it can provide an increased sense of purpose when our own life's compass might be wavering. Forbearance also can be used when considering the need to be patient while waiting for difficult times to pass and the return of more positive activities and influences within one's life.

We must all live our own lives in a healthy, balanced fashion to minimize the untoward effects of this demanding profession. Giving of ourselves, while honorable and uplifting, can be draining at times. Reflecting on our core values, beliefs, and ideals will help to maintain the balance needed. Forbearance helps buffer the times when we might feel a vacillation of our core.

Please don't mistake this suggestion of forbearance as a synonym for that old catchphrase of "just suck it up, grin and bear it." We all have already had our fair share of dosing on delayed gratification. Forbearance is much deeper. It is a philosophy (among many) that can help us stay connected to ourselves and to the worlds in which we choose to live. We all have a purpose and passion to which we resonate. The suggestion is to simply have forbearance as we each continue to seek those passions and purposes we cherish.

And for a real shift in your perspective on our importance and the need for some forbearance, take a look at this YouTube video from famed astronomer Carl Sagan: "Pale Blue Dot" at https://www.youtube.com/watch?v=GO5FwsblpT8. The hope is that you become uplifted and energized at a deeper level while you further consider how to be a better leader—to yourself and all those around you.

I encourage each of us to continue seeking deeper levels for how we continue to draw upon our beliefs in the qualities of professionalism, altruism, and forbearance. We can generate positive influence in this at all levels.

REFERENCE

1. Jonsen AR, with Braddock CH III and Edwards KA. Professionalism, University of Washington's "Ethics in Medicine" program. http://depts.washington.edu/bhdept/ethics-medicine/bioethics-topics/detail/75.

CHAPTER 23

Appreciation: Where Does It Lead?

Appreciation of others must necessarily be a critical aspect for leadership. Others must also be able to appreciate the nature and depth of leaders if mutual successes are to occur. The difficulty is that trust is earned and not presumed before others will open themselves to appreciate the leadership potential you or your team represent to those you are leading. We all need to appreciate this nuance so that our organization and practice environments can better succeed. Our patients will certainly appreciate the eventual outcome.

D
o you still remember and appreciate the moment when you decided to enter the field of medicine or your specialty discipline, and do you fully appreciate the change in professional directions you've created for yourself over time?

Chances are you trusted some internal instincts and then corroborated those with external inputs. Or maybe you just reacted in the moment, trusting all would work out eventually. Regardless, we all can appreciate those significant moments when we changed direction.

For me, going to medical school was a presumed pathway. My parents would deny it, but there was clear bias and strong indirect influence in their counseling for me to pursue this profession. Something about "how much you intuitively care for others. . ." was the catchphrase I remember most. However, it took me many years to appreciate that they were just looking out for my best interests—according to their values.

What I better appreciate though, is the moment I decided surgery was the optimal discipline for me. I was on a student rotation in a rural community with a small-town general surgeon. It was obvious patients loved him, other physicians respected him immensely, and he was clearly a community icon. There was something about his presence and the way he approached his work that was intangible but easy to appreciate.

Because of him, surgery itself was easy to appreciate. I intuitively learned for the first time that my thought processes and decision-making style were more compatible with surgery than with other clinical disciplines. It became a very simple choice. To this day, I appreciate the opportunity to have spent so many years in the field helping others through surgical practice.

Carl Jung once said, "With trust or loyalty to one's own experience, an individual had a solid base on which to build a life. Absent such experience, forced to rely on belief and faith, a person was liable to doubt, credulity and fear." From my perspective, trust and loyalty are an extension of appreciation of one's experiences. Continuing to acknowledge our life's trajectory, including its successes and setbacks, allows us to further appreciate how we can continue to better influence our own paths—paths that are pivotal for ongoing success as physician leaders.

So how do patients come to appreciate a physician or surgeon? What helps a leader become appreciated and trusted, enabling others to follow his or her direction with loyalty?

Sucher and Gupta penned an article in *Harvard Business Review,* "Leading with Trust."[1] They delineated how CEOs are hired " . . . to address high-stakes challenges and make tough decisions . . . their power rests on the willingness of the business's stakeholders to cede it to them . . . it depends a lot on stakeholders' trust." Five key dimensions are needed to engender ongoing trust for leaders at all levels:

1. **Legitimacy:** A leader is in that role for legitimate reasons and by a legitimate process.
2. **Competence:** A leader demonstrates skills well and is obviously good at that job.
3. **Motives:** A leader serves the interests of multiple stakeholders in a balanced fashion.
4. **Means:** A leader identifies the means needed to accomplish goals and sets the direction for an organization's actions. If those rules are perceived as fair, stakeholders will trust leaders and afford them appropriate power and loyalty.
5. **Impact:** A leader is judged on the impact created, regardless whether it was an impact that was planned or unintentional, positive or negative.

I have observed at conferences and in journals much commentary about trust—and the erosion of trust—in our industry. This is not a new topic of focus within healthcare. No doubt, we are undergoing unprecedented change, but complexity of healthcare is not a new issue, nor is the issue of whether trust is present.

Loyalty is pivotal on so many levels. Loyalty to yourself; loyalty to your family and friends; loyalty of others to you and your guidance; loyalty to your patients and patients' loyalty to you; loyalty of peers and coworkers; loyalty of your practice or organization's staff teams—the list can go on in many directions. There are volumes of research and literature on loyalty and the value it creates for individuals, patients, customers, and organizations. There even is a discipline of "loyalty-based management" that many follow. But loyalty and how it is generated is something we must all, as leaders, further understand and better appreciate for how it impacts others and our organizations.

In the corporate and association worlds, customers and members will remain loyal and keep buying or engaging only as long as they receive superior value and experiences; therefore, staff and employees must know how much value they are creating, if not individually, then as members of relatively small teams. Those in leadership must appreciate the potential for these levels of impact in either direction. These potential impacts are obvious for patient care as well.

In another significant piece, Wynia and Bedzow describe the importance of values-based leadership. In their article, "Values-Based Leadership During the Transformation of Health Care," published in *People + Strategy*, the authors describe how the changes occurring in healthcare are creating the potential for undermining healthcare's ethical foundations.[2] They posit that leaders must develop the skills necessary to give "voice" to the core values of healthcare. From their perspective, leaders must:

1. Recognize the competing ethical values underlying the challenges being faced.
2. Be competent in analyzing complex ethical dilemmas.
3. Learn to develop and implement realistic strategies that can maintain the core values of healthcare in a rapidly changing environment.

The article describes their Giving Voice to Values methodology to help leaders improve critical skills.

As individuals banding together, we can foster stronger leadership while maintaining core ethical values in addition to engendering trust and loyalty, a deeper appreciation for our past, present and future directions. It may also enable us, as leaders of varying size teams, to better appreciate the impacts we create across an organization. These impacts on our teams most often affect patient care delivery as well as healthcare delivery—directly and indirectly. These effects are related to values, trust, and loyalty of our society in the profession and the healthcare industry as a whole.

Leadership, although complex, is often about appreciating others and how they are influenced to achieve even greater outcomes by appreciating their own potential.

As you can now better recognize, appreciation in and of itself does actually lead somewhere. It helps reinforce ethical values, build trust, and engender loyalty—collectively creating value, optimizing experiences, and improving outcomes on several levels.

We must all continue to seek deeper levels of professional development and better appreciate how we can each generate positive influence at all levels.

WE WERE MADE FOR THESE TIMES

"Ours is not the task of fixing the entire world all at once, but of stretching out to mend the part of the world that is within our reach. Any small, calm thing that one soul can do to help another soul, to assist some portion of this poor suffering world, will help immensely. It is not given to us to know which acts or by whom, will cause the critical mass to tip toward an enduring good."

— Clarissa Pinkola Estes
Author, poet, and psychoanalyst

REFERENCES

1. Sucher SJ, Gupta S. Leading with trust. *Harvard Business Review.* July 17, 2019. https://hbr.org/2019/07/leading-with-trust.
2. Wynia M, Bedzow I. Values-based leadership during the transformation of health care. *People + Strategy.* 2019;42(3):23-33.

CHAPTER 24

Medicine, Human Wellness, and Ecology?

The healthcare workforce is always under duress and requires devotion to its own wellness. Paying attention to new developments in the science of medicine, as well as those developments occurring peripheral to the core of medical research, can challenge physicians in many ways. Getting back to the basics of improving human wellness is currently receiving a plethora of attention in the research community.

A t our core, we all want to feel safe, be healthy, stay happy, and be able to live our lives with ease and minimal discomfort. In spite of other desires, at our core, these four are pivotal.

Some days we forget just how privileged we are in life and become preoccupied with our unmet higher desires. Appreciating these simple core areas and purposefully choosing to be happy helps minimize the times when we feel our other wants are not being met.

We often need to find supplementary activities and information to help us meet these core needs. Mounting evidence suggests that getting physically in touch with nature can improve our overall health and wellness.

The evolution of medicine as a profession and as a provision of services to people is fascinating. For centuries, the primary focus of medicine has been on the diagnosis and management of diseases. Most assuredly, the pace of change in the past 120–150 years has been spectacular, and the capabilities for providing cures (or near cures) for numerous diseases is profound. Similarly, the pace of change with the advance of scientific research breakthroughs and the development of technologies moves along at a logarithmic scale. This duplicity of change, however, makes it attractive for the science of medicine to continue focusing on disease management and not on disease prevention.

Fortunately, the past decade has shown a gradual recognition and appreciation for the need to pay more attention to human wellness and disease prevention. What began with increased attention to so-called "alternative care" practices has now evolved into a full focus on human wellness, disease prevention, and even the fast-paced new focus on longevity. These budding areas of research and product development are filled with an extensive array of confusing literature and a variety of apostles.

The general public can be misled into excess spending on products based on marginal science. Popular magazines and many books are now profiling these benefits and helping readers collate the confusing sets of scientific evidence that are spread around in a variety of research disciplines and databases—not an easy accomplishment in the least, considering at recent count, there are nearly 500 scientifically published studies from around the world linking time in nature with better health.

For example, Dr. Qing Li, a professor at the Nippon Medical School in Tokyo, has demonstrated that trees and plants emit aromatic compounds called phytoncides that, when inhaled, can spur healthy biological changes in a manner similar to aromatherapy, which also has been studied for its therapeutic benefits. In his studies, Li has shown that when people walk through or stay overnight in forests, their blood often exhibits changes that are associated with protection against cancer, improved immunity, and lower blood pressure.[1]

Specifically, Li has studied natural killer immune cells, NK cells, that, like cortisol and hemoglobin, can be reliably measured in a laboratory. It's been known for a long time that factors like stress, aging, and pesticides can reduce a person's NK count, at least temporarily. So Li wanted to learn if nature, which reduces stress, could also increase our NK cells and thereby help humans fight infections or cancer.

Li brought a group of middle-aged Tokyo businessmen into the woods in 2008. For three days, they spent a couple of hours each morning hiking. By the end of the three days, their blood tests showed their NK cells had increased 40%. Moreover, the boost lasted for seven days. A month later, their NK count was still 15% higher than when they started. In contrast, during urban walking trips of the same duration, NK levels didn't change. Li also has published results from similar studies with male and female subjects while expanding the variety and type of chemical compounds exposed to or being monitored.[2]

In a recent breakthrough study, Hunter, Gillespie, and Chen measured biomarkers of physiological stress—salivary cortisol and salivary alpha-amylase—to quantify the change in physiological stress in response to the duration of exposure to nature.[3] The use of cortisol and amylase as biomarkers is predicated on being able to separate the nature exposure effect from the natural daily shift in production.

Both stress biomarkers indicated a reduction in stress response to a "nature experience" (NE). An NE resulted in a 21.3% per hour drop in cortisol beyond that of the hormone's 11.7% diurnal drop. The NE efficiency per time expended was greatest between 20 and 30 minutes, after which benefits continued to accrue, but at a reduced rate. For salivary alpha-amylase, there was a 28.1% per hour drop after adjusting for its diurnal increase of 3.5% per hour, but only for participants who were least active, sitting or sitting with some walking. It is the first study to employ long-term, repeated-measure assessment and the first evaluation wherein study participants are free to choose the time of day, duration, and the place of a NE in response to personal preference and changing daily schedules.[3]

Building off this evolving scientific literature, Dr. Robert Zarr, a pediatrician in the Washington, DC, area, is credited with starting the nonprofit Park Rx America program (www.parkrxamerica.org) that is gradually realizing success and gaining momentum with increasing efforts to have physicians write actual prescriptions for their patients to spend time outdoors in parks close to their homes—and then facilitate their ability to do so.

Leaders like Anne O'Neill of the National Park Service and Diana Allen with the Healthy Parks Healthy People program helped launch pilot initiatives in 2011 and 2013. Many other initiatives have been, or are now becoming active, around the world as well. For example, in 2006, there was one single U.S. nature prescription program; by 2018, there were 71 programs in 32 states, and 17 states that actively use the Park Rx app.[4,5]

But here is a frustrating paradox: Morale in the healthcare workforce is under duress due to increasing pressures from increased productivity pressures, encroachment of the electronic health record, decreasing reimbursements for care, and residual debt load from training. Providers of healthcare also must pay attention to the same sets of issues with which they assist their patients; physicians must make changes to their professional and personal lives in order to be healthier. The environments where patient care is delivered also must change in order to improve the quality of life for the public and the healthcare workforce.

So how does ecology fit into this picture? The definition I found most appealing for ecology is this: " . . . it is a branch of biology that deals with the distribution, abundance and interactions of living organisms at the level of communities, populations, and ecosystems, as well as at the global scale. Ecology is a broad science encompassing many fields."[6]

But now for another disturbing paradox: When researching the topic of ecology in a variety of online databases and coupling the term to other words like "medicine," "healthcare," "physicians," etc., what do you think shows up in those searches? Unfortunately, not much of anything!

The medical profession seems to be missing the opportunity to learn more about this area of critically important knowledge. However, it is always difficult to insert new or evolving topics into the medical school curriculum; and once out of medical school, fresh graduates have myriad issues and responsibilities to address as they gain specialty training and attempt to establish their clinical practices. So frankly, it is no wonder that peripheral topics such as ecology are not included in physicians' sphere of awareness during their professional lives.

As illustrated by the example of Park Rx mentioned earlier, however, we need strategies to increase medical professionals' awareness of the rapidly escalating importance of how we are affecting ecologies and, perhaps more importantly, how our ecology can positively affect humans and those who nurture and care for them. We still have much to learn.

By nature, physicians are high achievers. At our professional core, we all want to succeed in the science and art of medicine. We also want to continue moving toward mature approaches to true patient-centered care. These professional pursuits generally provide a great sense of satisfaction. However, at times, our evolving society and medical industry do not make it easy to remain optimistic, positive, and energized. For physicians, learning how to help ourselves, and how to continue better helping others, might be reframed in the context of broader societal challenges.

It is always appealing to simplify knowledge and theory, but we must recognize that we as human beings, living on this earth within the expanding awareness of our universe, are much more complicated when it comes to health, wellness, and longevity in the face of rapidly changing ecologies. Our challenges remain to create positive change and simultaneously to continue learning as best we can about minimizing negative influences on our environments. As it turns out, keeping our lives simpler while also getting out into nature can actually provide profound benefits to our lives.

The medical profession is complex and often has difficulty adjusting to external influences beyond the sciences of traditional medical research. Yet the varieties of research outside current medical research are showing benefits to human health in a variety of ways—some quite simple, others still more complex. Consequently, medical profession education is a lifelong process of professional development that must now assimilate additional information streams into the mainstream of clinical care.

REFERENCES

1. Li Q. Effect of forest bathing trips on human immune function. *Environmental Health and Preventive Medicine* 2010;15(1):9-17.
2. Li Q. Effects of phytoncide from trees on human natural killer cell function. *International Journal of Immunopathology and Pharmacology* 2009; 22(4):951-59.
3. Hunter M, Gillespie B, Chen SY-P. Urban nature experiences reduce stress in the context of daily life based on salivary biomarkers. *Front. Psychol* 10:722. doi: 10.3389/fpsyg.2019.00722.
4. Reuben A. Ask your doctor if nature is right for you. *Outside.* May 2019.
5. Williams F. *The Nature Fix: Why Nature Makes Us Happier, Healthier, and More Creative.* New York, NY: W.W. Norton & Company; 2017.
6. Ecology. Biology Dictionary. www.biology-online.org/dictionary/ecology.

CHAPTER 25

We Know About Physician Burnout; What About Physician Happiness

In our mission to support physician leaders, we continue to learn much about physician dissatisfaction. But unfortunately, we don't yet hear much about physician happiness, wellness, or career satisfaction.

I often mention this phrase because whether one pursues recognized leadership tracks or follows a career without formal leadership roles, those who enter the medical profession generally possess several natural leadership attributes such as:

- Intelligence;
- Altruism;
- Ambition;
- Motivation;
- Empathy;
- Adaptability;
- Integrity; and
- Decisiveness.

In addition, most all societies continue to expect that physicians display leadership traits, both clinically and in nonclinical life.

While physician leadership had recently become somewhat marginalized within the industry, with the recent flux in healthcare we now see physician leadership regaining significant recognition. Trends such as the integration of physicians as salaried employees in health systems, the emphasis on outcomes-based payment models, and the need to drive clinical care using evidence-based protocols have created a growing demand for dedicated physician leadership.

There is also an increase in physicians pursuing nontraditional career paths who seek advanced education and leadership training.

SHIFTING THE FOCUS TO PHYSICIAN HAPPINESS

In our mission to support physician leaders, we continue to learn much about physician dissatisfaction. But unfortunately, we don't yet hear much about physician happiness, wellness, or career satisfaction.

While burnout concerns are important and relevant, we must also begin to refocus ourselves and our profession toward the positive aspects of being a physician and reconnect with an improved appreciation for the profound benefits achievable with this career.

At the very least, we not only owe it to ourselves as individuals, but we also owe something to those entering the profession. The quality of medical student applications remains at very high levels as our profession continues to draw the "best of the best."

To help maintain the appeal of this profession to potential physicians, it is our collective responsibility to begin fostering an improved image of the physician career path as an opportunity for someone to become a satisfied, well-adjusted individual. There are certainly a multitude of pressures, and we must continue to recognize and prevent or manage physician burnout. But it is also time to bring attention to achieving physician wellness, happiness, and balanced lives.

As highlighted in a recent Shannon article, "Physician Well-being: A Powerful Way to Improve the Patient Experience," the five domains that predict physician dissatisfaction and the contributions to burnout identified in the Minimizing Error, Maximizing Outcome (MEMO) study are worth paying attention to so we can reflect on how they are impacting our lives.[1] More importantly perhaps, we should also consider how we can modify these influences so that we can turn negative impacts into positive outcomes.

Dissatisfaction domains:

1. Income
2. Relationships
3. Autonomy
4. Practice environment
5. Broader market environment

Contributions to burnout from MEMO study:

1. Time pressure
2. Work control
3. Work pace
4. Values alignment

STAYING BALANCED, DESPITE THE ODDS

Are physicians really that different from other professionals? Every profession has its stressors, and clearly those who make their livelihood outside of the professions have a host of stressors as well. And all people need to work hard if they want to succeed in our increasingly complex society. For everyone, the current global societal shifts can be complex enough by themselves. Comparatively speaking, perhaps physicians have just as many stressors as others.

And yet, there are some relatively unique aspects that differentiate our profession, including the protracted education tracks and the length of time it takes before physicians are established in their careers after formal training.

When you add in the stress of simultaneously trying to get a personal life off the ground, it's easy to see how a combination of these factors could potentially tip the balance unfavorably. Additionally, the deeply personal nature of caring for people creates unique responsibilities and higher levels of emotional stress when compared with other professions.

The steep trajectory and intensity at the beginning of physicians' careers often delays the opportunity for individual leadership skills to shine. As physicians progress through other career stages, those natural leadership aptitudes may actually continue to be suppressed if the balance has been shifted to the negative side of the satisfaction/dissatisfaction equation.

For me, the importance of finding how physicians can regain that balance—or better yet, proactively keep their balance—is an absolute necessity, not only for individuals but also for our profession as a whole.

We all ultimately aspire to personal happiness, however it is defined. As physicians and leaders in society, we have the potential to better demonstrate how we can take important steps to achieve that happiness. Personal happiness can also be like an infectious disease. As an individual you will affect not only your own life, but your family's life, your patients' lives, and all those around you. This is one type of infection we should learn better how to replicate, not eradicate.

REFERENCE

1. Shannon D. Physician well-being: a powerful way to improve the patient experience. *Physician Exec.* May/June 2013;39(4):6-8,10,12.

The Value of Physician Leadership

An extensive review of the literature, followed by dozens of interviews with health care leaders, confirms that matured physician leadership will be essential for health care to continue moving toward higher quality, consistent safety, streamlined efficiency and becoming value-based.

The healthcare industry has entered an era marked by seismic change and disruption of the status quo, and one area that is experiencing high demand and explosive growth is physician leadership.

Today, approximately 5 percent of hospital leaders are physicians, and that number is expected to increase rapidly as the health system moves toward value-based care.[1]

"The decade we're in is probably going to lead to the greatest amount of change that's been experienced for the last hundred years in health care," said Dean Gruner, MD, president and CEO of ThedaCare Inc., and a board member of the ThedaCare Center for Healthcare Value in Appleton, WI.[2]

Considering the rising rates of chronic disease, the growing physician and nurse shortages, and the aging of our population, the current environment presents outstanding opportunities for physicians to develop lasting improvements in care delivery. Overall, this represents a period of extraordinary opportunities for physicians to provide leadership.

A constellation of forces place physicians at the center of this stage:

- The shift from a volume-based to a value-based system.
- The public health-oriented focus on the management of populations toward wellness.
- The fundamental redesign of clinical care models in several settings.
- The financial payment models that have begun rewarding healthcare organizations for clinical excellence and coordinated care at reduced cost.
- The emerging shared risk, capitation and bundled payment strategies.

The fact that growing numbers of physicians are pursuing leadership positions bodes well for healthcare, according to Maureen Bisognano, president and CEO of the Institute for Healthcare Improvement in Cambridge, MA.

"It's a wonderful sign that physicians are expanding from clinical care to include learning what it takes to be a good leader," Bisognano said. "When you can marry the leadership skills and the clinical background, you have an opportunity to lead in a very distinct and different way. When you get someone who knows what quality looks like, and pair that with a curiosity about new ways to think about leading, you end up with people who are able to produce dramatic innovations in the field."

For several reasons, healthcare organizations need the distinctive perspective of physicians among their leadership. Because of increased constraints on revenue and heightened review by payers, health system leaders of today are now more often in the position of making administrative decisions that ultimately affect clinical care.

The American Association for Physician Leadership®, the nation's oldest and largest leadership education and career support organization for all types of physicians, champions the view that physicians are best suited to lead clinical efforts to achieve true patient-centered care. It is well-recognized that, at some level, all physicians are regarded by our society as leaders.

The association includes physician leadership as one of its nine essential elements required to provide optimal patient-centered care. The organization believes that, in order to succeed, healthcare must be: quality-centered, safe, streamlined, measured, evidence-based, value-driven, innovative, fair and equitable, and physician-led.

WHY PHYSICIANS?

Evidence suggests that organizations and patients benefit when physicians take on leadership roles. Physician leaders play critical roles in providing high-quality patient care. The 2013 U.S. News and World Report rankings for hospitals include an "Honor Roll" that lists 18 institutions. The top five are led by physicians, and 10 of the 18 are physician-led.[3]

Another study, *Physician leaders and hospital performance: Is there an association?*,[4] indicated that "the best-performing hospitals are led disproportionately by physicians." In each of three specialty areas—cancer, digestive disorders, and heart and heart surgery—"the better a hospital's performance, the more likely it is that its CEO is a physician and not a manager," the study found.

Specifically, the study found that overall hospital quality scores are 25 percent higher when doctors run hospitals. For cancer care, physician-run hospitals posted scores 33 percent higher than those run by nonphysicians.

A more recent investigation by the same author regarding business leadership in a highly competitive field outside medicine reached a similar conclusion: "Teams led by leaders with extensive knowledge of their core business perform better than others."[5]

Consultants with McKinsey & Co. conducted a study of factors associated with healthcare productivity. The researchers found an association between higher organizational scores on several management dimensions, with reduced rates of hospital-acquired infection and hospital readmission, greater patient satisfaction, and improved financial margins.[6]

The study revealed stronger physician leadership to be a key contributor to this organizational performance. The hospitals with greater degrees of physician leadership involvement scored higher, on average, in performance management and Lean management, and produced higher average overall management scores.

Physician leadership gives organizations "a competitive differential" and "a definite edge over a hospital that does not have it," noted Rick Guarino, MD, vice president of medical affairs of Wilson Medical Center in Wilson, NC, (then senior vice president and chief medical officer of Nash Health Care in Rocky Mount, NC) in American Medical News.[7]

INTERFACE PROFESSIONALS

Physician leaders provide that competitive differential because they have extensive knowledge about the "core business" of caring for human beings. They have learned, lived and breathed patient care.

"Having had that direct experience as a deliverer of care positions me to understand why, in my past medical practice, I may not have been as careful with attention to detail as I should have been," said Gerald B. Hickson, MD, senior vice president of quality, safety and risk prevention at Vanderbilt University Medical Center in Nashville, TN. "From a leadership standpoint, I experientially 'get it.' And that helps me collaborate with others to think about how we can encourage right delivery of care every time."

Physician leaders have been described as "interface professionals" who bridge medicine and management.[8] At the edge between other physicians and managers, physician leaders can be the catalyst that every successful organization needs, connecting the organization's so-called sharp end (the front lines of care) with the blunt end (related management, leadership and governance).[9, 10]

To foster that connection, Rutland Regional Medical Center (RRMC) in Rutland, VT, embraced a dyad model that pairs physicians and nonphysician administrators as co-leaders of services and programs. Several other health care organizations across the country have taken this approach as well.

According to Baxter C. Holland, MD, vice president of medical affairs at RRMC, "physicians are critical to the overall success of any healthcare organization, so to leave them out of significant leadership roles, you've basically tied one hand behind your back. You've also set yourself up for a 'we-they' dynamic if they are not part of the discussion. You can't really take them out of the equation and expect to achieve the improvements you are looking for."

With the right physician or physicians on the executive leadership team, the organization will be able to relate to non-physician managers as well as clinicians of several disciplines. Through the orders they place and the management they provide for patient care, physicians remain the primary drivers of care.[11]

For this reason, it's natural for physicians to be in key leadership roles shaping the decisions around what's best for patients and the organization.

THE SOUL OF THE BUSINESS

This, however, does not necessarily mean that physicians need to only be in titled leadership positions. Physicians of all types and in a variety of roles still provide leadership —albeit informal leadership.

It is natural that formal and informal clinician leaders tend to have attributes that are especially useful for health care leadership, including the belief fundamental to the art of medicine being "first, do no harm,"—an appreciation for the value of solid data and a receptiveness to evidence-based decision-making and an inclination to do "what's best for the patient."[12]

According to Cathy Wilkinson, MD, FAAP, chief personnel officer of Pediatric Associates Inc. PS, an 84-member practice headquartered in Bellevue, WA, that inclination helps physician leaders "understand the balance between the business reality and the reality of taking care of patients."

A nonphysician executive is more likely to be focused on the organization's financial success, she said. "At what cost do you do that? You can't scrimp on patient care or on morale and commitment to physicians and the rest of the health care team to make one more dollar. That's where the physician executive helps to bridge that gap in understanding."

Because they speak the same language and share common histories with most types of clinicians, physician leaders are more likely to empathize with the demands of their colleagues' clinical responsibilities and to make decisions sensitive to their needs, said Glenn Lux, MD, MBA, CEO of Pediatric Associates. "We understand the soul of the business because we've done it," he said.

According to Lux, the soul of their business means always putting the needs of patients first and doing so with consideration for the professional and personal lives of the clinical staff. "If we wanted just to be financially successful, we would have more doctors than we have now working weekends, we would have people working all night—and we would burn out our doctors," he said.

Lux believes the practice's physician leadership, which also includes a chief operations officer who is an MD, as well as a chief medical officer and a medical director at each of eight clinics, helps set the tone for a culture of respect, which in turn breeds satisfaction among the clinical staff and ultimately improves professional and financial performance.

"It's hard to give someone feedback if you don't know what they really do. That feedback is much more accepted from a physician than from a nonphysician who doesn't 'get it,'" he said. "When we ask our physicians to do something that's a little bit out of the ordinary, they know that we understand what that means to them and that we wouldn't ask unless it was important."

Having medical colleagues in administrative leadership positions helps to ensure that a medical practice remains focused on what is best for patients rather than primarily what is best financially, said Josephine L. Young, MD, MPH, chief operations officer for Pediatric Associates.

A physician is certainly not needed in every leadership role—the practice's CIO and CFO are not medical, she said. In fact, "there is value in having your senior leadership team come from a nonclinical perspective as well."

That blend of clinical and non-clinical backgrounds, including specialized expertise in information technology and finance, "allows you to treat the business side like a business and to draw from the best of both worlds," she said.

However, "because we're a medical practice, everything we do is ultimately related to the medical aspect. Having physician administrators takes that into account for decisions at every level. It's just inherently there," Young said. A nonclinical leader, even one with extensive healthcare knowledge, would not offer that same depth of understanding, she said.

For example, Young's knowledge of medicine contributed to the success of a recent operational discussion regarding complaints by some physicians about the schedulers' handling of bookings for consults. She drew on her clinical knowledge to present examples to facilitate the discussion, such as: Should a 15-year-old girl with a history of depression and chronic abdominal pain be scheduled as a consult or a sick visit?

"It was a split decision—the point being that you can't fault your schedulers for making the appointment, because you've got to do what the patient needs," she said. "It was a conversation stopper when I posed the question: 'If your best answer is "It depends," how is the scheduler supposed to make the decision? I played up the nuances to get my point across because I speak a common language."

When the H1N1 virus surfaced as a public health threat a few years back, Young's clinical knowledge enabled her to make key decisions more readily than if she had been a nonclinician.

"So many operational decisions needed to be made that hinged on information coming out of the Centers for Disease Control and Prevention regarding who should be vaccinated, who should get treatment, what clinical protocols to use and universal precautions. I was able to read through the health department recommendations, absorb the information and render a decision," she said.

Similarly, Heather Smith, MD, medical director of the hospitalist service at Rutland Regional Medical Center, uses her clinical knowledge and experience to support the hospital's corporate action plan to reduce length of stay and inpatient costs. To help achieve its objectives in these areas, the medical center has embedded clinical decision support in the electronic health record—an "added level of refinement" that provides physicians and nurses with access to a database of best practices, Smith said.

MATTERS OF TRUST

A shared history and a common language give physician leaders the credibility among their colleagues and other providers needed to garner critical support for clinical integration. This allows driving the value agenda for initiatives such as reducing variations in care, reducing readmissions, developing a patient-centered medical home, implementing best practices and other value-driven initiatives.

As a member of a multidisciplinary committee of medical directors and nonphysician leaders, including the chief financial officer, "What I bring to the table is the knowledge of how a physician uses this support and whether something will work. If you have these meetings in isolation, it takes so long to circle the wagons that by the time you get there, the best practices have already changed. It's much more efficient this way because it brings the clinical perspectives to the fore. My role is to identify the diagnoses we should tease out to be refined, and where we should put the links to our order sets" to make sure best practices are applied, she said.

"If you have physician leaders, you are more likely to have the medical staff follow the organization's direction," Holland said. "They're much more likely to follow other physicians than they are administrators."

And it's not just doctors listening to other doctors. Nurses, surgical technicians, nurse practitioners, physician assistants and all members of the direct health care team respect the physician's point of view and are more likely to buy into organizational changes led by the physician leader.

Recognition of that advantage by executive leadership served Baylor Health Care System (now Baylor Scott & White Health after a merger with Scott & White Healthcare in 2013) well in the formation of the BQA, the system's 2,600-member accountable care organization. Practitioners might have felt less confident about joining the organization had the hospital approached them directly, Lembcke said.

"The hospital helps supply the capital and resources, but a lot of the strategy and integration that has to occur is on the front load between the physicians," he said. "It takes an orthopedic surgeon leading the way to say, 'let's get together and choose the two [knee implants] that give the best cost and value.'"

As the BQA continues with clinical integration and markets itself to the community, it will take a physician to lead the discussions on how the physicians will be reimbursed. "You can't have the administration leading that discussion," Lembcke said.

To make sure physicians feel their voices are being heard, the leaders made a deliberate decision to create an organization whose board of managers consists primarily of physician leaders. This physician-led organization has begun to implement improvements to further the system's transition to accountable care.

The Best Care Clinical Integration Committee and 20 subcommittees representing specialties and subspecialties have so far developed 80 best practice protocols and processes with accompanying metrics.

A protocol for the treatment of uncomplicated low back pain was among the first chosen because it offered a relatively uncontroversial condition around which a multidisciplinary task force representing neurology, neurosurgery, physical medicine, pain, trauma medicine and rehabilitation could join forces. According to Lembcke, the Best Care Committee's next major task is making sure the data for the protocols are "well scrubbed" so they can be presented to the physician members.

RESPECTED CHANGE AGENTS

The respect and authority traditionally conferred on physicians helps them win support for change, both within their organizations and from the communities they serve. "Large-scale organizational changes . . . require strong leaders and a cultural context in which they can lead. For obvious reasons, such leaders gain additional leverage if they are physicians," said Thomas Lee, MD, former president of Partners HealthCare System in Boston, in Harvard Business Review.[13]

In an example of influence, the additional leverage provided by a physician leader enabled Rutland Regional Medical Center to win legislative and community support for the creation of a new six-bed acute care psychiatric unit. The unit has helped fill the significant services gap for individuals with severe mental illness, created when floodwaters from Hurricane Irene destroyed the 52-bed Vermont State Psychiatric Hospital in Waterbury in 2011.

The leadership of W. Gordon Frankle, MD, chief of psychiatry, helped the medical center obtain state resources to convert a portion of its inpatient psychiatric unit into a psychiatric ICU to care for some of the state's most seriously ill patients. The unit is one of a handful opened across the state to improve geographic access to short-term psychiatric care.

According to RRMC's Baxter Holland, Frankle served as an articulate and convincing spokesman for the hospital and advocate for effective treatment for people with mental illness. His professional standing as a psychiatrist and knowledge of the medical needs of individuals with severe psychiatric conditions gave the medical center an entrée and a degree of credibility among legislators, community members and other stakeholders that a nonphysician may not have had, he said. "People will listen when a doctor talks. They might not when someone else talks."

The credibility and trust engendered by a physician-led board and extensive physician committee structure have enabled the HealthTexas Provider Network to drive quality improvement since the multispecialty group's data-driven work in this area began in 1999.

The network of 633 employed physicians practicing in 211 sites throughout North Texas "has learned to trust the metrics once they are filtered by the physician committees and physician leaders," said F. David Winter, MD, MSc, MACP, president and chairman. Initially, physicians received blinded data on their performance relative to their peers. The network has gradually increased data transparency as a strategy to drive adherence with quality and safety core measures.

Today, unblinded data that ranks physicians according to quality metrics are shared transparently throughout the organization. "It took some time for the physicians to accept the data and to understand that change was coming," Winter said. "Now, we show them the data and they change. We have credible metrics. There's a lot of opportunity for improvement, but I think we're on top of getting the physicians to change as rapidly as possible to improve health care."

This physician influence can also be harnessed internally by involving peers in helping their fellow physicians reflect on feedback from patients and co-workers about problems and perceptions regarding their performance and professionalism.

A validated, tiered-intervention tool, the Patient Advocacy Reporting System®, developed by Hickson and his colleagues at Vanderbilt University Medical System, has reduced the institution's malpractice claims and losses by 80 percent in the past 15 years.

The reporting system, which has also been used by other hospitals and health systems, identifies disruptive behavior and uses data-informed peer interventions to improve self regulation by at-risk physicians.

"Research shows that the best way to do this is to have a physician [peer] who is actively engaged in helping other individuals change their own practices," Hickson said. "The goal is not to debate the merits of the data, but to ask the physician to reflect on why his or her performance is not where it should be. The good news is that the vast majority of people who get this feedback show improvement." [14]

TRANSITIONAL HURDLES

The need for physicians to serve as team builders, motivators, communicators and change agents has grown exponentially in a system that now recognizes healthcare organizations more for their medical performance than their operational acumen.

"As the complexities of healthcare reform take shape, more physicians will be called upon to lead the change. Who better to address challenges faced by health care organizations today than those with experience on the front lines?" said John R. Combes, MD, senior vice president of the American Hospital Association and president and chief operating office of the AHA's Center for Healthcare Governance.[15]

Although hospitals and health systems are scrambling to recruit talented candidates from the outside and to groom physician leaders internally with on-site courses, experiential learning opportunities, and certificate and advanced degree programs with universities and colleges, they have work to do in bringing physicians into the leadership fold.

According to a survey cited in the 2014 *American Hospital Association Environmental Scan,* 66 percent of health system CEOs report that physicians constitute only about one-tenth of their senior leadership teams. Only 52 percent of CEOs have a formal chief medical officer involved in strategic planning.[16]

"These are clinical issues, so you need clinical leadership to help guide the programs and implement the practices that will get you improved outcomes," Combes said. [17]

But physicians can't do it alone. They must work with professional clinical teams in a complex environment.

MULTIDISCIPLINARY TEAMS

Until recently, healthcare was primarily physician-centric and disease-focused. This focus has driven not only care delivery but also a majority of the business practices within the industry. A shift to team-based approaches and population health and wellness is occurring quickly. Those trains have clearly left the station, and physicians need to recognize these shifts.

Several healthcare organizations are already grappling with what this actually means and how to successfully implement team-based clinical care. There are a variety of initiatives around the country and the world aimed at moving the industry toward multi-professional and interprofessional team-based education.

A new horizon is slowly approaching. Pride in being a physician who is passionate about quality patient care is a professional expectation grounded in centuries of behavior. The pride and passion for the physician "team" will not be easily displaced—nor should it.

Yet the world is rapidly changing, and the physician workforce must continue to change as well. Other clinical disciplines and non-clinical professionals also have pride and passion for their respective disciplines. They, too, want to work at the "top of their license."

Although the association has a legacy of promoting physician-led care and physician-led teams, the organization recognizes the importance of the changing environment and highly respects each of the nonphysician disciplines active in health care delivery.

Specifically, the association has active initiatives or is in serious discussions with several nonphysician disciplines, including nursing, pharmacists, financial managers, nonclinical administrators, the legal community, healthcare researchers and information management professionals, to emphasize a team-based approach to care.

The entire healthcare industry is ultimately about patient-centered care. This is one common factor for which every discipline has true pride and passion. Healthcare professionals are all playing on the same team for patients, regardless of which discipline or model of care delivery they support.

For a variety of reasons, many physicians have a tendency toward autonomy and independence. However, it is important to recognize that this behavior can create misperceptions and impediments, directly and indirectly, to successful patient care outcomes. It also can create barriers to forming, leading or participating in successful teams.

It is critical that physicians develop deeper insights into how this behavior might have become engrained in their attitudes and how it could be modulated and channeled in a positive fashion—without losing their pride and passion.

The association believes it will take some time for formal medical education programs to foster different behaviors in the student and resident population, but those changes are occurring. It also will, therefore, take time for the current physician workforce to gradually adjust to initiating and promoting collaboration and partnering.

In the interim, the association supports the idea that balanced physician leadership behaviors could and should begin to emerge that will promulgate a transition from command and- control behaviors to an atmosphere of collaboration and success for all members of a team or organization.

NEW INTELLIGENCE NEEDED

Physicians still have work to do. They must acquire a new set of competencies, including team-building and communication skills, and the business intelligence in finance, marketing, strategy formulation, information technology, law and other areas required to steer health care organizations of all sizes over the bumps and pitfalls of a complex system in flux.

As James L. Reinertsen, MD, of the Reinertsen Group, Alta, WY, said, "Physician leadership roles are powerful potential leverage points for improvement of the health care system. As citizens in the health care system, physicians have an obligation to learn as much as possible about effective leadership so that when an opportunity to lead comes, they will make optimal use of it."[18]

Among other things, physician leaders need financial literacy "to link the quality of care with the financial resources they're expending to produce that quality," noted Bisognano of the IHI. They must be able to speak the language of and connect fluently with boards of trustees, insurers, senior executives, clinical chairs and chiefs, patients, and staff. "The same person needs a sense of each culture," she said.

To prepare for these expanded roles, Richard J. Gilfillan, MD, president and CEO of CHE Trinity Health, headquartered in Livonia, MI, and former director of the federal Center for Medicare and Medicaid Innovation, urged physicians to "learn as much as you can about the nonclinical areas," such as finance, operations and IT, "and how the pieces come together. I believe that exposing yourself to as much of the organizational activity as possible makes you a richer contributor to the leadership team." This deeper understanding produces leaders who can "think synergistically with the other disciplines about how to optimize across multiple dimensions," he said.

Toward that end, the physician leadership development program at CHE Trinity Health focuses on enabling physicians to "broaden their framework for thinking about health care" by learning about the other key disciplines, such as marketing, strategic planning and law, said Donald Bignotti, MD, senior vice president and chief medical officer.

The program challenges physicians to "absorb the nonclinical side of the world and then come back and think about how it fits into the world of delivering health care," he said. That experience prepares physicians to serve as part of a larger team.

ADJUSTING TO AMBIGUITY

There is no dearth of leadership potential within the physician talent pool. Physicians come to the table with multiple finely tuned skills and strengths.

Noted Jason Petros of Witt/Kieffer in Oakbrook, IL, physicians are "intrinsically fast learners, are extremely outcome driven, have high expectations and an unparalleled work ethic. They are comfortable with responsibility and decision making. In other words, they already have executive leadership skills. These attributes have made them successful in solo practices or small team environments, and can be leveraged for success in the executive suite."[19]

Despite these assets, physicians often encounter obstacles in making the transition from clinical to leadership responsibilities. The two worlds differ significantly.

Much of the difficulty stems from the autonomous problem-solving and authoritative decision-making abilities drummed into physicians during medical school and residency training. That training does not lend itself to the large-picture, vision-oriented, collaborative approach required to develop strategy, instigate clinical integration, and motivate teams, hospitals and systems to produce sustainable improvement.

"As a result, when physicians transition to a leadership role, they sometimes try to take the same approach to management problems that they took to medical problems," said Stephanie Sloan, PhD, and Rod Fralicx, PhD, of Hay Group in H&HN Daily.

"Rather than coaching and helping others solve problems, they might try to jump in and fix those problems themselves. If their team is not performing as well as they would like, some physician leaders respond by doubling their own efforts to model the type of behavior they would like their fellow physicians to emulate. Independent problem solving may serve physicians well during surgery, but it does not necessarily deliver as a leadership tactic." [20]

That prescribing, fix-it-now tendency can stifle the cultural momentum needed for transformation. There is cultural value and power in learning when to step back, said Hickson of Vanderbilt.

"People come to me, and I might know what they need to do, but if I allow them to reflect and come to their own opinion, it is their success, and it sustains the effort," he said. "When medical leaders go out and try to fix other people, and they don't get fixed, they provide a 'push back': 'But I just did what you told me to do.' This is the downside of physicians who haven't changed the way they approach problems."

An individual with an episodic, problem-solving mindset does not always adjust easily to the ambiguity and delayed gratification that are virtually inevitable aspects of hospital and health system leadership. And it may actually take years for a physician to unlearn their historical behaviors as they a tempt to adopt newer behaviors that are better appreciated in nonclinical environments.

"We [physicians] don't always spend the time needed to understand all of the nuances of the problems of a complex health care organization—problems that can be even more challenging, in their own way, than the human body," James E. LaBelle, MD, corporate senior vice president and chief medical officer of Scripps Health in San Diego, observed in Healthcare Executive. [21]

Noted Hickson, "The hardest thing I have had to do in my career is to learn that I cannot fix every single human's problem. I have to create a system that allows them to reflect, develop insight and solve their own problems. A significant issue with some medical leaders is that they can never make that transition."

MANAGEMENT IS NOT LEADERSHIP

Gilfillan made that transition by cultivating a "servant leader" leadership style that emphasizes the modeling of honesty and integrity and helping others find their own way to become more effective. Those supportive behaviors "lead to a culture that people get excited about and perform their best in," he said.

It can be done, but the leap between worlds requires mental gymnastics. Delos Cosgrove, MD, president and CEO of Cleveland Clinic, noted in Business Insider that losing the immediacy of quickly knowing the impact of a decision he had made in the operating room was the biggest change he faced when he became a physician leader. As an executive, "You make a decision and you may find out two years later," he said.[22]

The proclivity to act and to do can predispose physicians to confuse management with leadership and to emphasize the acquisition and use of management skills at the expense of developing a unifying and inspiring sense of purpose, according to Joseph S. Bujak, MD, co-author of *Leading Transformational Change: The Physician-Executive Partnership*[23] and author of *Inside the Physician Mind: Finding Common Ground With Doctors.* [24]

Although physician leaders need proficiency in both realms, they also need to understand the differences between the two. "Martin Luther King, Jr. had an 'I have a dream' speech, not an 'I have a plan' speech," Bujak said. "The 'plan' is management. The dream without the plan gets you nowhere. But the plan without the dream becomes about what you do, and people don't care about what you do. They care about why you do it. Leadership is about why you do it. What aligns people is that sense of commitment to shared purpose, and what binds them together is the covenant that says this is how we will behave and hold each other accountable."

Many physicians also make the mistake of assuming clinical skill translates into leadership ability, Bisognano said. The two do not always go hand in hand. "Clinical skills are certainly a requirement, but they are not enough. It's about vision and strategy and moving a system culturally toward the Triple Aim" of better health, better care and lower cost.

"That's very different from solving problems one at a time. It requires a different tempo of decision-making, a different scope of work and a different set of skills," she said.

In Executive Insight, consultant James A. Rice, PhD, FACHE, of Management Sciences for Health in Medford, MA, encouraged physician leaders to focus more time and energy on developing those skills. This involves a shift in focus from hard skills, such as technical competence and clinical expertise, to soft skills, such as building relationships and emotional intelligence.

The change can pose challenges for professionals who receive "little, if any, exposure to formal assessment and training in establishing effective interpersonal skills" and whose careers have "focused on functioning in an independent, decisive and dictatorial manner," he said.[25]

A qualitative analysis of physician leadership behavior at eight primary care practices underscored the interpersonal skills challenges physicians may face. The study zeroed in on the attribute of inclusiveness.

"Some physicians may intellectually understand what it means to practice leadership inclusiveness, and even believe that they are doing so, when in fact, they may actually be undermining the collaboration they are aiming to support," observed Jenna Howard, PhD, and her colleagues at the Robert Wood Johnson Medical School, New Brunswick, NJ.

They noted that inclusive leadership requires both an invitation to others to participate and an expression of appreciation for that participation with a positive and constructive response. "It may not be enough for professional organizations and researchers to simply encourage physician leaders to practice leadership inclusiveness. Rather, such an approach likely needs to be explicitly taught and supported." [26]

INNOVATIONS IN EDUCATION

Medical educators and healthcare organizations have begun working to help physicians address these and other shortfalls. Recognizing that a dictatorial manner can hinder patient safety by inhibiting important information-sharing and discussions with nurses and other members of the patient care team, WellStar Health System in Marietta, GA, includes mandatory physician training in inclusive leadership as part of a comprehensive patient safety program.

Launched in 2008, the physician-led training is designed to help physicians understand how their behavior as care team leaders impacts patient safety. The program has helped achieve an aggregate

80 percent reduction in high-level safety events across the system and improve scores on the Patient Safety Culture Surveys of the Agency for Healthcare Research and Quality and the Gallup Employee Engagement survey.

In addition to providing training in safety science, the program heightens physicians' sensitivity to behavioral cues and signals that can help or hinder free and open communication among members of the care team.

"The physician has an important role in promoting an environment that leads to high-performance teams and allows members to feel comfortable about asking questions and raising concerns," said Marcia L. Delk, MD, senior vice president of safety and quality and chief quality officer.

Toward this end, for example, physicians learn to encourage team members to communicate their observations and concerns and to respond in an accepting and inclusive manner when those concerns are raised. "Intimidating or demeaning a person who asks a question sends the wrong signal and can lead to oversights and errors that jeopardize patient safety," Delk said. "The goal is to embed these skills in the culture and have physicians hard-wire awareness of these behavioral cues in their leadership skill set."

Similarly, the American College of Osteopathic Internists has developed a training program, the Phoenix Physician, to help primary care residents and practicing physicians develop skill in delivering high-quality care with respect for patients as members of the care team.

In addition to training physicians in using performance metrics and information technology to measure and improve care, the program incorporates leadership and communication skills training and helps physicians develop an appreciation for the contributions of all team members.[27]

The organization's efforts have impacted physicians and healthcare in various ways.

"Doctors must recognize the unique skills required to be effective physician leaders and the necessity for continuous adult learning. The association is an essential ingredient in the journey to becoming a successful physician executive," said Scott Ransom, DO, MBA, MPH, FACOG, FACHE, CPE, FACPE, of Fort Worth, TX.

"A CMO must possess many tools. To ensure my role as a successful physician leader, I have learned that additional training is no longer an option—it's a prerequisite," agreed Robert Bratton, MD, CPE, FAAFP, CMO of Lexington, KY.

To involve physicians very early in their training in teamwork and communication around projects that lead to real and sustained outcomes improvement, the Texas A&M Health Science Center College of Medicine has formed a House Staff Quality and Patient Safety Council for interns and residents who are completing their clinical training through a joint program with Baylor University Medical Center.

The recently formed council, whose purpose is to function as a liaison between the house staff, the Graduate Medical Education Committee and the institution, is expected to provide "a proving ground for leadership," said Cristie Columbus, MD, vice dean of the program and assistant director of medical education at BUMC.

"All of our residents receive training in teamwork and communication, but the House Staff Council will be the most well-developed avenue by which resident leaders will emerge and participate in the life of the institution."

CORE COMPETENCIES FOR LEADERSHIP EXCELLENCE – WHAT QUALITIES, SKILLS, AND ATTRIBUTED DO PHYSICIAN LEADERS NEED TO LEAD WELL?

The Healthcare Leadership Alliance, a six-member, multi-professional collaborative consisting of the Association and five other professional advocacy groups (the American College of Healthcare Executives, the American Organization of Nurse Executives, the Healthcare Financial Management Association, the Healthcare Information and Management Systems Society, and the Medical Group Management Association), has created a list of 300 competencies required for effective healthcare leaders.

The 300 competencies are grouped into five primary competency areas:

1. **Knowledge of the healthcare environment** — The understanding of the healthcare system and the environment in which health care managers and providers function.

2. **Professionalism** — The ability to align personal and organizational conduct with ethical and professional standards that include a responsibility to the patient and community, a service orientation, and a commitment to lifelong learning and improvement.

3. **Communication and relationship management** — The ability to communicate clearly and concisely with internal and external customers, establish and maintain relationships, and facilitate constructive interactions with individuals and groups.

4. **Business skills and knowledge** — The ability to apply business principles, including systems thinking, to the healthcare environment.

5. **Leadership** — The ability to inspire individual and organizational excellence, create and attain a shared vision, and successfully manage change to attain the organization's strategic ends and successful performance. [28]

Likewise, in *Exceptional Leadership, 16 Critical Competencies for Healthcare Executives,* [29] Carson F. Dye, MBA, FACHE, of Witt/Kieffer, and Andrew N. Garman, PsyD, MS, of Rush University in Chicago, put forward a similar list of the core qualities and attributes that most commonly distinguish the highest-performing health care leaders.

With findings based on an extensive literature review, a review of competency lists prepared by boards and executives for executive searches, and surveys and interviews with healthcare executives and search consultants, Dye and Garman organize the 16 competencies into four cornerstones:

Well-cultivated self-awareness: An understanding of one's strengths, limitations, hot buttons and blind spots.

Compelling vision: The capacity to create effective plans for an organization's future.

Real way with people: Skill in listening, giving feedback, mentoring, developing champion teams and energizing staff.

Masterful style of execution: The ability to generate informal power, build consensus, make decisions, drive results, stimulate creativity and cultivate adaptability.

The most effective leadership development training takes place by doing and by learning under some type of pressure, according to Dye. He advocated a three-pronged approach to leadership development that stresses a 70-20-10 blend of challenging assignments, relationships, networking and feedback from mentors and peers, and formal training.[29]

The "crucible" experiences that involve obstacles and pressure force leaders "to examine who they are, what matters to them and what they can learn from success and failure," he said.

A FRAMEWORK FOR CHANGE

In a 2013 white paper, *High-Impact Leadership: Improve Care, Improve the Health of Populations, and Reduce Costs,*[30] the Institute for Healthcare Improvement presented a three-pronged model for health care leaders at all levels to support the transition from volume-based to value-based care. The model encompasses the following dimensions:

- Individuals and families are partners in their care.

- Compete on value, with continuous reduction in operating cost.
- Reorganize services to align with new payment systems.
- Everyone is an improver: Everyone in the organization should see themselves as having two jobs: to do their work and to improve their work.

High-impact leadership behaviors:

- Person-centeredness: Be consistently person-centered in word and deed.
- Front line engagement: Be a regular, authentic presence at the front line and a visible champion of improvement.
- Relentless focus: Remain focused on the vision and strategy.
- Transparency: Require transparency about results, progress, aims, and defects.
- Boundarylessness: Encourage and practice systems thinking and collaboration across boundaries.

The association's Meta-Leadership courses and certificate target many of those specific behaviors. People who are able to work across systems to engage people and get them working together — Meta-Leaders — are much more effective within their organizations and from career perspectives.

Meta-Leadership is composed of five dimensions that define outstanding leadership:

The person of the Meta-Leader: Ability to understand one's own emotional intelligence, weaknesses, biases and strengths so that one can lead with balance, discipline and direction.

Situational awareness: Ability to accurately comprehend the situation or problem—even when full information is unavailable.

Leading the silo: Ability to empower co-workers to achieve maximum effectiveness.

Leading up: Ability to educate and help superiors understand what is happening so they can make good decisions.

Leading across: Ability to connect and inspire disparate stake-holders, departments/silos and other organizations to work together to accomplish a mission.

CONCLUSION

Clearly, the need for physician leaders is great, and the value they bring to healthcare organizations is significant. One recent example comes from reports from the Centers for Medicare and Medicaid Services (CMS) where it reported on the first year of experience with accountable care organizations (ACOs) and how physician leadership made a positive impact. According to the CMS data:

Of the original 114 ACOs from the program's first year, only 54 were able to successfully attain their targets.

Of those 54, 29 ACOs successfully received their added bonuses.

21 of those 29 ACOs that received bonuses were physician-led.

And 29 percent of physician-led ACOs achieved savings greater than their minimum savings rate, versus 20 percent of the remaining participants (mainly hospital sponsored).

Overall, physician-led ACOs tend to be more nimble in execution of their programs than hospitals—e.g., improvements in care coordination, chronic disease management and prevention.

Other examples are notable from a variety of settings, but clearly physicians, with their deep clinical understanding and desire to provide the best care for patients, are well-placed to help bring about the redesign of care that is the bedrock of health reform. Matured physician leaders are able to further leverage their skills and provide even deeper levels of expertise to the evolving heath care industry's reform processes.

"Nobody went to medical school, nursing school or business school to deliver fragmented, unaffordable care. Everybody went because they wanted to do great things for patients, families and communities," said Gilfillan of CHE Trinity Health.

Physician leadership is critical to shepherd health care into the future, creating a delivery system grounded in better health and better health care at lower costs.

This special report was first published by the American Association for Physician Leadership® in April, 2016.

REFERENCES

1. Physician Leadership Education, American Hospital Association's Physician Leadership Forum, 2014.

2. Insight Magazine WI, January 29, 2013 http://www.youtube.com/watch?v=7oxCSLeoBgc

3. U.S. News and World Report, July 16,2013, http://health.usnews.com/health-news/best-hospitals/articies/2013/07/16/best-hospitals-2013-14-overview-and-honor-roll.

4. Goodall AH. Physician-leaders and hospital performance: Is there an association? Social Science & Medicine, Elsevier, vol. 73(4), 535-539, August 2011.

5. Goodall AH, Pogrebna, G. Expert Leaders in a Fast-Moving Environment, IZA Discussion Papers 6715, 2012, Institute for the Study of Labor (IZA).

6. Mountford J, Webb C. When clinicians lead. The McKinsey Quarterly. McKinsey & Company, London. 2009.

7. Stagg Elliott V. Hospitals ramp up training for physician leadership roles. American Medical News, February 23, 2012. Available at http://www.amednews.com/article/20120223/business/302239997/8/. Accessed March 12, 2014.

8. Kaiser LR. Key management skills for the physician executive. In: Curry W, Linney BJ, eds. Essentials of Medical Management. American College of Physician Executives. Tampa, FL; 2003:11-33.

9. Cook RI, Woods DD. Operating at the Sharp End: The Complexity of Human Error. In: Bogner MS, ed. Human Error in Medicine. Hillsdale, NH: Erlbaum and Associates; 1994:255-310.

10. Reason J. Managing the Risk of Organizational Accidents. Hampshire, UK: Ashgate Publishing; 1997.

11. Birk S. The future of physician leadership: physician leaders and the changing healthcare landscape. Healthcare Executive, 28(1):8-16, January/February 2013.

12. Silbaugh BR, Leider HL. Physician leadership is key to creating a safer, more reliable health care system. [ACPE white paper] PEJ. 35(5):12-8, September/October. 2009.

13. Lee TH. Turning doctors into leaders. Harvard Business Review. April 2010. Available at: http://hbr.org/2010/04/turning-doctors-into-leaders/ar/1. Accessed March 12, 2014.

14. Pichert JW, Moore IN. An intervention model that promotes accountability: peer messengers and patient/family complaints. Jt Comm J Qual Patient Saf. 39(10):435-46, October 2013.

15. Combes JR. Physician leadership: the implications for a transformed delivery system. Hosp Health Netw. 88(2):12, February 2014.

16. 2014 American Hospital Association Environmental Scan. Hosp Health Netw. 87(9):51-3, 55-8, 60-1, September 2013.

17. Stempniak M. Value-based leadership. Is your hospital management team prepared for the future? Hosp Health Netw. 87(5):41-8, 1, May 2013.

18. Reinertsen JL. Physicians as leaders in the improvement of health care systems. Ann Intern Med. 128(10):833-8, May 15, 1998.

19. Petros J. Becoming a physician executive: suggestions for taking the next natural step. Witt and Wisdom: The Witt/Kieffer Executive Leadership Blog, October 23, 2012. Available at https://www.wittkieffer.com/webfoo/wp-content/uploads/Becoming-a-Physician-Exec-Suggestions-for-Taking-the-Natural-Next-Step.pdf Accessed March 12, 2014.

20. Sloan S., Fralicx, R. The new power players: influential physician leaders will shape the future of health care. H & HN Daily, June 16, 2011, Health Forum. Available at: http://www.haygroup.com/downloads/us/6_16_11_HHN_Daily_%282%29.pdf Accessed March 12, 2014.

21. Birk S. Creating a culture of 'we': investing in physician leaders. Healthcare Executive, 29(1);10-18, January/February 2014.

22. Nisen M. Big changes are coming for the U.S. healthcare system. Business Inside, December 25, 2012.

23. Atchison TA, Bujak JS. Leading Transformational Change: The Physician-Executive Partnership. Health Administration Press, Chicago, IL, 2001.

24. Bujak JS. Inside the Physician Mind: Finding Common Ground With Doctors. Health Administration Press, 2008.

25. Rice, JA. Expanding the need for physician leaders. Executive Insight, Advance Healthcare Network, November 16, 2011. Available at: http://healthcare-executive-insight.advanceweb.com/Features/Articles/Expandingthe-Need-for-Physician-Leaders.aspx Accessed March 12, 2014.

26. Howard J, Shaw EK. Physicians as inclusive leaders: insights from a participatory quality improvement intervention. Qual Manag Health Care. (3):135-45, Jul-Sep 2012.

27. Good RG, Bulger JB. The Phoenix physician: defining a pathway toward leadership in patient-centered care. J Am Osteopath Assoc. 112(8):518-20, Aug. 2012.

28. Combes JR, Arespacochaga E. Lifelong Learning: Physician Competency Development, American Hospital Association, Chicago, IL, 2012.

29. Dye CF, Garman, AN. Exceptional Leadership: 16 Critical Competencies for Healthcare Executives. Health Administration Press, Chicago, IL, 2006.

30. Swensen S, Pugh M. High-Impact Leadership: Improve Care, Improve the Health of Populations, and Reduce Costs. IHI white paper: Institute for Healthcare Improvement, Cambridge, MA. 2013. (Available at ihi.org)

About the American Association for Physician Leadership®

The American Association for Physician Leadership (AAPL) believes all physicians are leaders and recognizes that society still has this expectation of physicians.

AAPL maximizes the potential of interprofessional, physician leadership to help create personal and organizational transformations that benefit patient outcomes, improve workforce wellness, and refine the delivery of healthcare internationally.

Since its founding in 1975, AAPL has remained the only healthcare organization solely focused on providing full-service professional development offerings, leadership education, and management training oriented toward the physician workforce and the organizations where physicians work or are represented. AAPL is home to the well-recognized, industry-standard Certified Physician Executive (CPE) credential.

For more information, visit www.physicianleaders.org

Hear Dr. Peter Angood's podcast at:

https://www.soundpracticepodcast.com/e/why-physicians-must-lead-change-all-physicians-are-leaders/

American Association for
PHYSICIAN LEADERSHIP

www.ingramcontent.com/pod-product-compliance
Lightning Source LLC
Chambersburg PA
CBHW070401200326
41518CB00011B/2018